ECONOMIC ANALYSIS
IN TALMUDIC LITERATURE

STUDIA POST-BIBLICA

GENERAL EDITOR

DAVID S. KATZ (Tel Aviv)

ADVISORY EDITORS

ITHAMAR GRUENWALD (Tel Aviv)
FERGUS MILLAR (Oxford)

VOLUME 40

ECONOMIC ANALYSIS IN TALMUDIC LITERATURE

Rabbinic Thought in the Light of Modern Economics

BY

ROMAN A. OHRENSTEIN

AND

BARRY GORDON

E.J. BRILL

LEIDEN • NEW YORK • KÖLN

1992

The paper in this book meets the guidelines for permanence and durability of the Committee on Production Guidelines for Book Longevity of the Council on Library Resources.

Library of Congress Cataloging-in-Publication Data

Ohrenstein, Roman A.
   Economic analysis in Talmudic literature: rabbinic thought in the
light of modern economics / by Roman A. Ohrenstein and Barry Gordon.
      p.   cm.—(Studia post-Biblica, ISSN 0169-9717; v. 40)
   Includes bibliographical references (p.   ) and index.
   ISBN 9004095403 (alk. paper)
   1. Economics—Religious aspects—Judaism.   2. Talmud—Criticism,
interpretation, etc.   I. Gordon, Barry (Barry Lewis John)
II. Title. III. Series.
BM509.E27038   1992
296.1'206—dc20   91-41392
                                                            CIP

ISSN   0169-9717
ISBN   90 04 09540 3

PRINTED IN THE NETHERLANDS

With All My Love to, my dear wife Ruth, my grandchildren, Jennifer-Josefa and Scott-Shalom, and their parents, Gena and Jeff Hollander, and to my younger daughter Ilana Rose Ohrenstein

To my daughter, Ruth Margaret Gordon

B.G.

R.A.O.

CONTENTS

ACKNOWLEDGEMENTS

We are indebted to the following publishers for permission to reproduce and/or paraphrase the material from the below listed works published by them:

American Journal of Economic Sociology, New York, N.Y. U.S.A.

ROMAN A. OHRENSTEIN. "Economic Thought in Talmudic Literature in the Light of Modern Economics". Copyright 1968.
ROMAN A. OHRENSTEIN. "Economic Self-interest and Social Progress in Talmudic Literature". Copyright 1970.
ROMAN A. OHRENSTEIN. "Economic Analysis in Talmudic Literature: Some Ancient Studies of Value". Copyright 1979. (Also published by the "American Society for Information Science" in Microfishe). Copyright 1980.

International Journal of Social Economics (Incorporating, *The International Review of Economics and Ethics*), MCB University Press, Bradford, West Yorkshire, England.

ROMAN A. OHRENSTEIN. "Value Analysis in Talmudic Literature in the Light of Modern Economics". Copyright 1986.
ROMAN A. OHRENSTEIN & BARRY GORDON. "Some Aspects of Human Capital in Talmudic Literature". Copyright 1987.
ROMAN A. OHRENSTEIN & BARRY GORDON. "Quantitative Dimensions of Human Capital Analysis in Talmudic Tradition". Copyright 1989.
ROMAN A. OHRENSTEIN. "Game Theory in the Talmud – An Economic Perspective". Copyright 1989.
ROMAN A. OHRENSTEIN & BARRY GORDON. "Risk, Uncertainty and Expectation" Copyright 1991.

Nassau Review, Garden City, N.Y. U.S.A.

ROMAN A. OHRENSTEIN. "Some Studies of Value in Talmudic Literature in the Light of Modern Economics". Copyright 1981.

PREFACE

BY

DAVID WEISS HALIVNI

The study of classical Jewish texts has enjoyed a revival, even a renascence, in recent times, both in the State of Israel and in Jewish communities of the Diaspora. Through both traditional and contemporary approaches, these texts have been rediscovered as the still relevant, still challenging sources of Jewish practice, identity and piety. Indeed, "back to the sources" has been the motto of those who have returned to the Torah, Talmud and Midrash with vigor and dedication. This activity has reflected not only a renewed commitment and attachment to an ancient Jewish preoccupation, but has constituted, quite concretely, a retrieval of the Jewish past. Out of the ashes of the Holocaust, in which the great centers of Torah knowledge were destroyed, has emerged a phoenix of Jewish learning. And in Jewish terms, learning represents living.

The cornerstone of Jewish learning has traditionally been the Talmud, and it has reemerged as the nucleus of this generation's intellectual and religious interest. The Talmud is the storehouse of Jewish law and lore, and has functioned as both the practical guide to Jewish observance and the inspiration to Jewish theology. In it is contained Jewish wisdom pertaining to virtually all aspects and domains of human life, elucidating the relationship between man and God and regulating the interaction of man and his fellow man. No realm of human endeavor is left ungoverned or unilluminated, as the compass of Talmudic learning is broad and its profundity deep. For these reasons, the Talmud has survived as the textual embodiment of the Jewish spirit, and is still being tapped today as the wellspring of Jewish spirituality.

In its encyclopedic coverage of both the mundane and sublime elements of human existence, the Talmud certainly does not ignore man's economic pursuits. Economics becomes part of the integrated system of Jewish law, in which conventional categories of sacred and profane are largely irrelevant. Economics is not classified as secular and therefore excluded from the purview of Talmudic discussion. The Rabbis of the Talmud possessed a comprehensive, all-embracing religious vision of human life, and therefore prescriptions and proscriptions relating to labor, business, damages, and commerce are naturally and necessarily components of Talmudic legislation. Economics is consecrated through Rabbinic analyses of various features of man's economic life, precisely because man, in his role as economic actor, is not excused from first clarifying and then obeying God's will. The Talmud has much to say about economic issues because economics has much of a say in human behavior. The scholar of Talmudic law becomes by necessity well versed in economic matters because the latter represents an important subset of the former.

There are, however, few people who can bring to the study of traditional Rabbinic literature an expertise in modern economic theory, or who can contribute to the increasingly useful field of modern economics through the perspective of traditional Jewish learning. The scholar is rare who can be regarded as an authority in both Talmudic law and economic theory, who has been reared on a diet of Jewish study yet also trained in the academic science of modern economics. Professor Roman Ohrenstein is such a scholar, and with his co-author Professor Barry Gordon, has produced a pioneering work in which the analytical tools of modern economic theory are proved efficacious in the understanding of Talmudic economic concepts, and in which those Talmudic concepts are demonstrated to be relevant to the clarification and refinement of modern economic theories. The unique Talmudic concept of a "valueless value" and the Talmud's superimposition on its game theory the ethical doctrine of *Bitzzu'a*, are, a.o., cases in point. In *Economic Analysis in Talmudic Literature: Rabbinic Thought in the Light of Modern Economics*, the worlds of yeshiva learning and academic social science converge productively and profitably, with benefit to both tributaries of knowledge. Professor Ohrenstein, a survivor of the Holocaust, is himself a symbol of the regeneration of Jewish learning in the late twentieth century and a purveyor of its riches, and this book an emblem of the fruitful encounter of traditionalism and modernity.

D.W. HALIVNI
Professor of Talmud and
Classical Rabbinic Literature
Department of Religion
Columbia University, New York

PREFACE

BY

JOHN C. O'BRIEN

It is with great pleasure that I write the preface to this original book by Professors Ohrenstein and Gordon. I am acquainted with both authors; Professor Ohrenstein I know well. Dr. Roman A. Ohrenstein and I first met when he presented a research paper in a session entitled *Issues in Economic Thought*, at the 55th annual conference of the Western Economic Association, San Diego, California, June 19, 1980. As a participant in this session, I was particularly impressed with Dr. Ohrenstein's presentation of his paper: "Some Studies of Value in Talmudic Literature." The study of values in our society today is of overriding importance. It is also a very controversial issue, especially in the social sciences. With remarkable foresight and perspicacity, Dr. Ohrenstein grasped this nettle at least a decade ago within my ken alone. Part four of the present work is devoted to "The Values of Persons."

Since that time, Dr. Ohrenstein and I have met at various conventions where he has pursued his studies in Talmudic literature, firm in the belief that there was much in these writings that could provide us with the guidance we need in this day and age when those values which have perdured the test of time are not only rejected but derided. In this present work, however, Dr. Ohrenstein and Dr. Gordon have concentrated on the role of Talmudic literature in economic analysis. This book is the fruit of their concentrated labor over the decade just ending.

In 1983, at the Third World Congress of Social Economics held in Fresno, California, August 16–20, Professor Ohrenstein was the chairman of a session entitled *The Talmud and the Economic Order*. His co-author of this present work, Professor Barry Gordon, an Australian, produced a paper called "Economic Welfare and Regulation of the Economy in the Pentateuch." Three years later these two Talmudic scholars cooperated to write: "Some Aspects of Human Capital" in a session entitled *The Socio-Economic World View in Judaic Thought*, at the Fourth World Congress of Social Economics, Toronto, Canada, August 12–15, 1986.

More recently, the present writer and Dr. Ohrenstein participated in a session entitled *Ethics and Economics* of the First Congress of the International Society for the Intercommunications of New Ideas (ISINI) held at the University of Paris, Sorbonne IV, August 27–29, 1990. Professor Ohrenstein had some advice for his fellow economists in his most edifying paper: "Risk, Uncertainty, and Expectations in Talmudic Literature."

Together with his colleague, Dr. Gordon, Dr. Ohrenstein has throughout the last decade labored diligently in the vineyard of the Talmud to produce the present original work. Besides serving as an introduction to Talmudic literature, this highly original book has something new to say to all economists. For the specialist in macro-economics, there are sections devoted to social progress, to scarcity and to business fluctuations. For him who has chosen to labor in the field of micro-economics, there are chapters dealing not only with opportunity cost, risk and uncertainty, but also with game theory and the Talmudic Minimax with an ethical quality superimposed upon it. The social economist who eschews the mainstream economist's *wertfrei* approach to problems in the economic and social order, as well as the specialist in the history of economic thought, will find much food for thought in this work, but especially in the last two parts of the book which are devoted to Talmudic literature on *The Values of Persons* and on the *Impact on Western Economics*. A few comments of the present writer will be directed at these later parts of this text which happen to appeal to him as a social economist.

The Talmud, "a body of Jewish literature encompassing an entire civilization" (p. 1), has much to offer us in these days when a slightly nervous finger might press the button that consigns humanity to extinction. Economic values, although theoretically subject to ethical principles, are, nevertheless of fundamental importance. What war, one might ask, does not have economic values somewhere at its roots? This work is of course directed at economists, but the subject matter of the Talmud includes "law, ethics, history, economics, medicine, philosophy, science, mathematics, theology and folklore." (Ibid.) It is from such writings as these that we mortals should turn to in these parlous times. The authors of the present work have done just that in their endeavor to find "answers" to the problems that beset today's civilization, problems with which our present day leaders appear unable to cope. Professors Gordon and Ohrenstein have certainly pointed out a path that economists today might do well to tread and, indeed, to follow to the end.

Adam Smith's *The Wealth of Nations*, 1776, and his concept of the invisible hand would find support in the writings of the Talmudic scholars. Not only does the Talmud argument rest on majority rule but it showed a concern for "norms of individual behavior conducive to a good and satisfying life for that person, and to the community well-being . . ." (p. 17). The wisdom of which our authors write acknowledged a divine order shaping the affairs of mankind, but since much of its emphasis was secular, utilitarian and humanistic, a new wisdom was born whose task was that of "bringing the world and man back into the centre of God's sphere of activity . . . All wisdom is from God, and is the Torah." (Ibid).

The present work indeliberately provides an answer to what German economists called *das Adamsmithproblem*. In his great work of 1776, Adam Smith described the doctrine of self-interest in the economic order with these words: "It is not from the benevolence of the butcher, the brewer, or the baker that we expect our dinner, but from their regard to their own interest. We address ourselves not to their humanity but to their self-love, . . ." (*The Wealth of Nations*, Modern Library, p. 14) This view puzzled German economists when they contrasted it with something Smith had written some seventeen years earlier: "And hence it is, that to feel much for others, and little for ourselves, that to restrain our selfish, and to indulge our benevolent, affections, constitutes the perfection of human nature, . . ." (*The Theory of Moral Sentiments*, August M. Kelley, Publishers, p. 27).

The Talmud provides the answer to *das Adamsmithproblem* in *The Fable of the Evil Impulse*. The fable's underlying message, (recounted, pp. 43–46), is that "mankind has been endowed with two diametrically opposed impulses. These two 'souls', the spiritual and the mundane, the virtuous and the vicious – are present in each individual and are designed to compete constantly with one another." (p. 45). In these Talmudic writings, our authors see not only the solution to the problem in the writings of Adam Smith which bothered German scholars, but they also point to a link betwen the teachings of the Talmud, Adam Smith's emphasis on self-interest, and Bernard Mandeville's *The Fable of the Bees*, 1705.

Of particular interest to this writer were chapters eight and ten, entitled respectively, "Categories of Value" and "Jews in the European Economy." Under the subheading of *The Doctrine of a Valueless Value*, the following observation appears: "The ethical connotation of this analysis is explicit. In the realm of ultimate values, there is to be no distinction between the physically fit and the disfigured, between the healthy and the handicapped. Nor . . . between saint and sinner, learned and simple . . ." (p. 134). It is remarkable that this wisdom of the Talmudic scholars is to be found in the work of a recent Viennese Thomistic philosopher, Johannes Messner: *Social Ethics*: Natural Law in the Western World. Professor Messner wrote: ". . . we must seek in reason the ground for the excellence perfection, and full reality of human existence. If this were not true, a cripple would have to be regarded as bad intrinsically, an idea which calls forth an emphatic protest. Indeed, we know that in a cripple's personality, essential humanity can be much more fully realized than in a man who is wholly sound in body. It is, then, in and through the mind that man is man in accordance with the requirement of the full reality of his nature." (p. 16).

In the final chapter is examined the extent to which concepts from Talmudic literature may have influenced the development in Europe of the social science that economics was to become. Through a discussion of usury and high finance, the authors arrive at a discussion of capitalism and the role of the Jews in its development. Here the social economist and the specialist in the history of economic thought will find a stimulus to further endeavor. Not everything on the origin of capitalism has been written by Max Weber or Werner Sombart or R. H. Tawney.

In this text, the prominent works of Max Weber and Werner Sombart are briefly discussed. In contrast to Weber who emphasized the link between modern capitalism and the Protestant Reformation, the role of the Jews was emphasized by Sombart "who was particularly impressed by the sophisticated character of the economic analysis of the *Talmud*." (p. 166). Sombart saw in the modern capitalist a life impelled by the pursuit of gain, *das Erwerbsprinzip*, as opposed to the medieval scheme of things where economic activity was rooted in the pursuit of consumer satisfaction, *die Bedarfsdeckung*. The pursuit of gain, *das Erwerbsprinzip*, Sombart regarded as Judaic rather than Puritan. Sombart's thesis that the Judaic foundations of European capitalism were subsequently extended to the United States has been attacked by a number of Jewish scholars, one of whom, Salo Baron, found it "brilliant" but "undisciplined." (*Ibid.*)

The final subsection here is called *The Spanish Connection* giving a note of modernity to a historical account of the Jewish experience in Spain. This subsection is no less enlightening than the preceding one. In medieval Spain, we learn, Jews lived under both Christian and Moslem rule. Yet, many prospered, rose to positions of power, and "were widely accepted in secular professional ranks." (p. 168). Under these conditions, it is not surprising therefore that many a Talmudic scholar made his contribution to the literature from his domicile in Spain. With the expulsion of the Jews from Spain in the late fourteenth century, the precise influence of Talmudic literature and thought in Europe became difficult to follow. As a result of this event, our authors express the hope that in the "evolution of Spanish economic thought we will find one of the main conduits through which Talmudic thought flowed into the West." (p. 171). It is to be hoped.

This fine, scholarly work is certain to give all economists palatable food for thought. It directs our attention to many areas of study in which much research still remains to be done. It certainly emphasizes, unwittingly or not, the importance of values in the economic order. It will assuredly whet the appetite of the true scholar, whatever his calling, who sees in the pursuit of knowledge an end in itself. The authors of this text, Professors Ohrenstein and Gordon, engaged in such a pursuit. They are to be warmly congratulated for the production of this impartial and disinterested study. I commend them.

JOHN C. O'BRIEN PH. D.
Professor of Ethics and Economics
California State University, Fresno

PREFACE

BY

ROMAN A. OHRENSTEIN and BARRY GORDON

Economics, as we know it today, began to take shape in Europe during the eighteenth century. Yet, economic analysis has a much longer lineage. Such analysis may be found in the writings of the ancient Greek philosophers, Islamic scholars, medieval Schoolmen, and the Mercantilists of the sixteenth and seventeenth centuries. The literature of ancient China, as well as that of India, also provides instances.

There exists, however, a vast, ancient Jewish literature which contains a wealth of analytical insights on economic issues. This Jewish contribution has been subject to little scientific investigation in the light of modern Economics. The predominant source of that contribution is found in the surviving writings of antique Jewish civilization – the *Talmud*.

Through study of the original dialectics of the *Talmud*, the present authors have been able to discern a wide range of economic discussions which display an extraordinary degree of sophistication when viewed from either contemporary or modern perspectives. Some of these discussions are extensive in scope, singular in approach, analytic in method, and profound as to insight. Sections of the *Talmud*, and the reflections of subsequent commentators on those passages, are rich in concepts and in statements of functional relationships that were later to become significant in the reasoning of the political economists or that of their professional-academic successors.

It is in this latter sense that the talmudic tradition embodies thought which can be said to "anticipate" later developments. This is not to claim that economists, modern or contemporary, have drawn consciously on talmudic sources. Nor is it to claim that Economics as a discipline was conceived, or even contemplated, by the rabbis. These latter were concerned with matters legal, moral, and theological, as were later the medieval scholastics. Nevertheless, in the process of investigating some of those matters they were led to insights that were to emerge again in a new disciplinary context. This book attempts to identify certain of those insights. Its findings are intended to be of interest to students of the history of economic thought and of the *Talmud*, as well as to the general reader in the broad field of the history of ideas.

Part One of the book is devoted to background analyses. The opening chapter is designed for readers unfamiliar with the *Talmud*, and it offers an introduction to that work's scope and development, plus some illustrations of its methodology. The second chapter outlines the biblical background to talmudic economic analysis, with particular reference to economic observations in the Wisdom tradition, and to the economic content of the legal codes contained in the Torah (Pentateuch). Both the Wisdom tradition and the law codes were vital elements in the intellectual milieu which gave rise to the talmudic tradition. As such, they provided points of departure for aspects of rabbinic debate.

Parts Two, Three and Four take up particular issues in economic analysis, and then compare the relevant talmudic treatments of them with those that correspond in the literature of Economics. Part Two deals with questions of macro-economic significance. In Part Three, the focus is on micro-economic matters. Part Four is devoted to the economic implications of the rabbinic treatment of the values of persons. Finally, in Part Five we turn to the question of whether or not talmudic insights may have had an impact on the evolution of economic thought and practice in the West.

The foregoing are supplemented by an Appendix which lists related modern studies. This bibliography is intended as an aid to further research. It includes publications by historians of economic thought, plus other items that could prove helpful to workers in this field.

The present volume is the result of research by the authors over some thirty years. During that time, we have benefited greatly from the assistance and encouragement of a number of scholars. In particular we wish to acknowledge our debt to Professor David Weiss Halivni, Professor of Talmud and Classical Rabbinic Literature, Columbia University, New York; and Head of a rabbinical academy (Rosh M'Tivta), The Institute of Traditional Judaism. Professor Halivni, a foremost Talmudic scholar, has given of his time and expertise in helping us resolve certain questions regarding difficult talmudic passages. In addition, he has kindly consented to enhance this book with a Foreword.

The authors are also greatly indebted to Professor John C. O'Brien, Professor of Ethics and Economics, California State University, Fresno, California. For many years, Professor O'Brien, a distinguished Social Economist, has been in the forefront of those promoting the type of research of which the present volume is one example. We are grateful indeed for the valuable perspectives which his Foreword provide.

Amongst the other scholars whose assistance has been of immense benefit, we would like to thank, in particular, Dr. Will Lissner, Editor-in-Chief, *American Journal of Economics and Sociology*; Dr. Paul Hait, Executive Vice-President, New York Board of Rabbis; and Dr. Stephen Moresh, City University of New York. We also acknowledge our debt to former teachers and friends; the late Dr. Arthur F. Burns (Columbia University, New York); the late Dr. Tzemach Tzamrion (University of Haifa); and the late Dr. Philip Alstat (Jewish Theological Seminary of America). In addition, we wish to thank the present editors of the *International Journal of Social Economics*, the *Nassau Review*, and the *American Journal of Economics and Sociology* who have granted permission for the authors to draw on material first published in these periodicals.

The manuscript was typed, in the main, by members of the Secretarial staff of the Department of Economics, University of Newcastle, New South Wales. We are most grateful for the support of Miss Elizabeth Williams, Mrs. Lorraine King and their colleagues.

R.A.O.
B.G.

PART ONE

BACKGROUNDS

CHAPTER ONE
THE TALMUD AND ITS METHOD

The Talmud (Hebrew: "learning") is a body of Jewish literature encompassing an entire civilization. It embodies the intellectual labours of ancient Jewish teachers in Palestinian and Babylonian Jewish academies from the third century BCE to the fifth century of our calendar. The efforts of the scholars over the eight hundred years involved were directed in particular at the exposition and development of the religious, moral and civil law of the Hebrew scriptures. The result was the erection of a vast storehouse of knowledge and information. In the Talmud, almost every facet of human endeavour is reflected. The subjects of talmudic discourse include law, ethics, history, economics, medicine, philosophy, science, mathematics, theology and folklore, among many others.

There are two Talmudim: the Palestinian (Jerushalmi, ca. 100 BCE–425 CE) and the Babylonian (ca. 300 BCE–500 CE). Of the two, the Babylonian, which was edited some fifteen hundred years ago, is the fuller and more systematic.[1] The text consists of approximately two and one half million words on some 5,894 folio pages. About one-third of the text is *Halakha* (legal) and two-thirds *Aggada* (narrative). Since Aramaic was the language of discourse, even among scholars, over the period concerned, both Talmudim are in Aramaic. However, each employs a different dialect.

Within the Talmud, there are two main sections: *the Mishnah* (legal code, edited ca. 220 CE), and *Gemara* ("study"). These are supplemented by some additional laws called *Baraitot*. The *Mishnah* ("repetition") is a book of laws developed by the sages in Eretz-Israel, called *Tannaim*. Whereas, the *Gemara* is the work of later sages both of Eretz-Israel and Babylonia, called *Amoraim*. The title *Amora* is derived from Hebrew *amar*, meaning "to speak", to interpret. It is a class of talmudic authorities who lived after the final redaction of the *Mishnah*, thus adding a second element to the development of the oral law. Eventually, the *Mishnah* and *Gemara* were combined in one work, and the word "Talmud" came into use as an appellation of the whole work.

---

[1] For the Babylonian Talmud, see, *Talmud Bavli*, Rom edition (Vilno, 1911). An English translation is *The Talmud*, edited by Isadore Epstein (Soncino Press, 1938). There are other editions and translations.

The Babylonian and Jerusalem Talmuds are essentially the interpretation and elaboration of the *Mishnah* as it was carried on in the great academies of Babylon and Eretz-Israel. There is no real difference between the Palestinian and Babylonian Amoraim. The distinction is merely chronological. The two groups were in close contact through frequent visits. Other writings by the sages left out of the Talmud, such as *Tosefta* ("Additions") supplementing the *Mishnah*, as well as *Midrash* (textual exposition of legal and non-legal teachings), are also part of the Talmudic spectrum.

The Origin of the Talmudic Tradition

There exists an ancient authoritative Jewish tradition that both the Written Law and the Oral Law were received by Moses at Sinai. This two-fold Torah has been known as *Torah She-be-Ketav* ("The Torah in Writing") and *Torah Shebeal-pe* (a "Torah orally transmitted"). Both the Book and the oral tradition were carefully preserved and transmitted from generation to generation. A traditional chronological record of the origin and transmission of the oral tradition in Judaism states:

> Moses received the Torah on Sinai and handed it down to Joshua; Joshua to the elders; the elders to the prophets; and the Prophets handed it down to the Men of the Great Assembly.[2]

When viewed from a historical perspective, there is a sound basis for the existence of an oral tradition along with the Written Law. Other ancient peoples entertained similar notions. Sophocles, for instance, refers to "the immutable unwritten laws" as he made Antigone justify the burying of Polynices against the order of King Creon, claiming that these laws "were not born today nor yesterday: they die not and none knoweth whence they sprang". And Aristotle in his *Rhetoric* spoke of written and unwritten laws. The latter, he said, were based on nature and universally recognized laws.

Similar distinctions were made by Philo (ca. 25 BCE–40 CE) and particularly by Josephus Flavius (ca. 38 CE–100 CE). Josephus wrote:

> By the side of Scripture there had always gone an unwritten Torah, in part interpreting . . . the written Torah, in part supplementing it. The existence of such a tradition in all ages is indubitable.[3]

---

[2] *Mishnah* ABOT, I:1 The *Mishnah* (300 BCE–200 CE) opens with this statement to emphasize its veracity and originality.
[3] See, Josephus, *Antiquities of the Jews*, XIII, 10:6.

Accordingly, in the writings of the Prophets and in the Hagiographa which are part of the Hebrew Bible, we find references to laws and customs that are not found in the Pentateuch. Such statements are recorded in Jeremiah 32:9–12; Ruth 4:5; II Kings 4:1, and in other places. Sometimes the text itself puts those events in a historical frame of reference by specifying that the given custom had been handed down from time immemorial: ". . . from former times in Israel" (Ruth 4:7). This, then, is a clear indication of the primordial existence of an oral tradition.

The same is evident from the Mishnaic treatment of the Pentateuchal law *lex talonis* of retributive justice: "an eye for an eye, a tooth for a tooth". (Ex. 21:24–25). Written as if in shorthand, the Mishnah (B.K. 8:1) takes it for granted that the law "an eye for an eye" refers to monetary compensation. No source is cited to prove it. The *Tannaim* found it unnecessary to justify its interpretation of the same, for this—they felt—has always been the oral understanding of the Mosaic law. The Mishnah records the oral law as a matter of fact.

Inasmuch as the Torah (Pentateuch) contains both explicit and implicit laws, often presented in concise fashion, these laws were subject to interpretation and elucidation. Naturally, during periods of cultural and economic changes, this became even more pronounced. Thus, after the destruction of the first Temple in Jerusalem in 586 BCE and the ensuing Babylonian exile, the Jewish people were confronted with new challenges in the religio-cultural sphere as well as in the socio-economic domain. The foreign environment along with the Zoroastrian customs and mores, necessitated a novel approach to the new demands of life.

Even a greater challenge was presented by the campaigns of Alexander the Great in Eastern Mediteranean. The powerful cultural upheaval and the economic changes which were wrought in its wake, called for a new strategy, even reforms, in the face of new conditions and requirements. That vital function was carried out by the *Sopherim*, "Scribes", who were not only copyists of the Torah, but also its interpreters. The founder of the *Sopherim* was "Ezra the Scribe", (5th cent, BCE). As a royal scribe of priestly descent, he was responsible for a series of religious reforms and for laying the foundation of the new Judean Commonwealth. The Talmud ascribes to him, a.o., the final decision on the text of the Pentateuch and the introduction of the Hebrew script. He flourished at the critical period of transition from the prophetic to the pharisaic era which marks the start of the formation of the Talmud.

There followed a succession of Scribes and Sages from whose ranks came the "Men of the Great Assembly". They went one step beyond interpreting the law by instituting *Takkanot* (or "enactments") and *Gezeirot* (edicts) not derived from the Torah. Though they were made mainly for the purpose of protecting the Law, these were nevertheless emendations of the biblical text based on the oral tradition.

This process came to full fruition during the latter part of the Second Temple period when the *Sanhedrin*, a term derived from the Greek *synedrion*, meaning "council court", was inaugurated in 141 BCE. The *Sanhedrin*—a legislative and educative body—went a notch beyond the "Men of the Great Synod". To be sure they continued to interpret the Law and issued ordinances, as the Men of the Great Synod did. However, they also incorporated old laws into statutory laws which in turn served as a basis for new laws to bring them into consonance with contemporary life. Moreover, in doing so, they kept the law fluid and dynamic.

In fact, the Sanhedrin subscribed to the progressive views of the Pharisees. According to Josephus, the Pharisees recognized the oral law as binding, whereas their contemporaries—the Sadducees—did not. The former saw a need for interpretation of the Pentateuch in the light of the new requirements, the latter denied the same. The Sadducees were, therefore, static in their approach; they were opposed to adaptability and eventually disappeared. By contrast, the Pharisees were dynamic in their outlook, as manifested in their discussions and dialectical reasoning. The upshot of those debates came to be known as *Halakhah*, the Hebrew root of which is *halokh*, to walk, to be in motion like a stream in constant flow.[4] It can be affirmed that the *Halakhah* responded to the wider demands of Judaism and life so as to meet the new challenges and problems in the spheres of the social, economic, political and theological.

In this latter connection it should be noted that the Second Commonwealth of Judea, particularly in the later period, was not functioning in splendid isolation. Rather, it was greatly affected by cultural notions stemming from Hellenism. These had to be addressed and dealt with. It is clear then, that the talmudic literature in the making was not merely a Jewish affair, but was also intimately bound up with the entire Greco-Roman world.[5]

---

[4] For a penetrating analysis of the theological side of the dispute, see Louis Finkelstein *The Pharisees*, (Philadelphia: Jewish Publication Society of America, 1962), Vol. II, pp. 762–79.

[5] See, Saul Lieberman, *Greek in Jewish Palestine* (New York: Jewish Theological

The Talmudic Method

A basic characteristic of the Talmud is that its method is dialectical and its approach is analytical. The dialectics are marked by interminable discussions, argument and counter-arguments. Theories are advanced and contradicted. These are followed by refutations, qualifications and clarifications. As for its analysis, it is framed within a set of rules and regulations founded on inductive and/or deductive reasoning.

The oldest rule promulgated by Hillel (first century BCE) consists of "seven principles: *Kal-vehomer*—"inference from minor to major", or "from major to minor". This is followed by the *Gzera-shava*— "inference by analogy". In passing from the inductive to the deductive categories, there is the rule of *K'lal u'Prat* and *Prat u-Klal*—a general proposition followed by a specifying particular, and a particular followed by a general. Whereas the former is in the category of inductive reasoning, the latter is one of scientific deduction. Later, R. Ishmael (first-second century CE) amplified the same to "thirteen principles of interpretations."[6]

Mention should also be made, however briefly, that because of the enormously complicated text of the Talmud which is by no means of one fabric, there is not one authoritarian version, but innumerable variant readings of it. In fact, textual criticism of the Talmud is as old as the Talmud itself. In modern times, however, it became a separate scholarly concern, where scientific method is applied to correct corrupt and incomprehensible passages.[7]

As noted above, a basic characteristic of the Babylonian Talmud is the analytical sharpness and ingenuity with which a subject is examined and crystallized. Every phrase, every word, even syllable is carefully probed and weighted. Accordingly, there is nothing superfluous in the Mishnah. If something appears to be redundant, there must be a reason for it and that reason must be found. Though disjointed and unsystematized as it may sometimes

---

Seminary, 1942); *Hellenism in Jewish Palestine*, (New York: Jewish Theological Seminary, 1950); "Palestine in the Third and Fourth Centuries", *JOR*, Vol. 36–37, 1946.

[6] Midrash *Sifra*, ch. 1 Introduction. The *Sifra* originated in Eretz-Israel during the second century CE and was compiled at the end of the fourth century when the Jerusalem talmud was completed. For a study in depth on hermeneutic rules, see, S. Lieberman, *Hellenism in Jewish Palestine* (New York: Jewish Theological Seminary of America, 1950), pp. 52–82.

[7] See, in particular, D. Weiss-Halivni, *Sources and Traditions*, Vol. I (Tel-Aviv, Dviv Publishers, 1968) and Vol. II (Jewish Theological Seminary of America, 1975).

appear, the "rabbinic mind" is coordinated by a complex of "value concepts", rooted in concrete human experience and woven into the fabric of life.[8]

Another noteworthy feature of the Talmud is that it is primarily concerned with finding and understanding the truth. Its emphasis is not on acceptance, but on understanding. Although the Talmud to this very day is the primary source of Jewish law, it cannot be cited as an authority for the purpose of ruling.[9] The Rabbis expressed opposing views as they attempted to interpret the law. Yet, the final decision was rarely pronounced. Rather, decision was left to history and practical experience, to be hammered out by succeeding generations of Rabbinic scholars in accordance with the changing requirements of life. That emphasis is clearly manifested in the Rabbinic literature that followed the Talmud, and it continues to this very day.[10]

Talmudic Argument Illustrated

An introductory chapter does not lend itself to a detailed analysis of the vastness and depth of the Talmudic spectrum. Hence, we shall limit ourselves to a few examples to illustrate the nature and method of Talmudic controversy.

The following episode recorded in the Talmud is filled with drama and suspense. The story is presented in a legendary fashion and revolves around a heated debate between R. Eliezer and the Sages concerning a stove of a certain construct. Is the stove ritually clean or unclean? R. Eliezer declares it clean and the Sages unclean.[11]

> It has been taught: On that day, R. Eliezer brought forward every imaginable argument but they (the Sages) did not accept them; (whereupon he said), 'if the *Halakha* (the law) agrees with me, let the carob-tree prove it.' Thereupon the carob-tree was torn a hundred cubits.' No proof can be brought from a carob-tree—they retorted. Again, he said to them: 'If the *Halakha* agrees with me let the stream of water prove it!' Whereupon the stream of water flowed backwards.

---

[8] See M. Kadushin, *The Rabbinic Mind* (Jewish Theological Seminary of America, New York, 1952), pp. 97ff.

[9] For additional explanation see "Encyclopedia Judaica", Vol. 15, pp. 750–78. See also *The Essential Talmud* by Adin Steinsalz, tr. from Hebrew by Ch. Galai, (Basic Books, Inc. Publ., New York, 1976).

[10] See in particular, *A Tree of Life: Diversity, Flexibility, and Creativity in Jewish Law*, by Louis Jacobs (Oxford University Press, 1984).

[11] *Baba Mezia*, 59b. Translated into English with notes, glossary and indices . . . under the editorship of Rabbi Dr. I. Epstein, London. (The Soncino Press, 1962).

'No proof can be brought from a stream of water'—they rejoined.
Again, he urged: 'if the *Halakha* agrees with me let the walls of the
schoolhouse prove it'. Whereupon the walls inclined to fall. But R.
Joshua rebuked them, saying: 'When scholars are engaged in an
halakhic dispute, what have ye to interfere? Hence, they did not fall in
honour of R. Joshua, nor did they resume the upright in honour of R.
Eliezer: and they are still standing thus inclined. Again, he said to
them: 'If the *Halakha* agrees with me, let it be proved from Heaven!'
Whereupon a Heavenly Voice cried out: 'Why do you dispute with R.
Eliezer, seeing that in all matters the *Halakha* agrees with him!' But
R. Joshua arose and exclaimed: 'It is not in Heaven' (Deut.
XXX:12). 'What did he mean by this?' Said R. Jeremiah: 'that the
Torah had already been given on Mount Sinai: we pay no attention
to a Heavenly Voice in matters of *Halakha*, because Thou hast long
since written in the Torah at Mount Sinai: 'After the majority must
one incline.' (Ex. 23:2).

This remarkable story illustrates one of the major characteristics of
the Talmudic method. In matters of *Halakha*, human reasoning is
asserted to be independent. The declaration that the Torah is no
longer in Heaven, and that a Heavenly Echo or other sort of
"miracle" cannot serve as proof if it is contrary to human reason, is
considered of paramount importance.

Furthermore, the story suggests that if the sharpness of an argument is employed in a manner as if to tear out a tree from the
ground or to prevent a stream from running its natural course, or to
destroy a schoolhouse, it is deemed to be contrary to good common
sense. The game must be played according to the rules. In matters
of halakhic dispute the *majority view* must prevail. The Torah is
"The Law of Life," manifested in the *Halakha* which responds to
life's situations and demands.

As the above story continues metaphorically, it emerges the
question was not yet fully resolved. In order to ascertain the
complete veracity of the majority view, further investigation was
still required. Only after receiving unqualified confirmation of their
position on this matter, did the majority decide to discipline R.
Eliezer for insubordination. Though R. Eliezer was an intellectual
giant, he accepted his censure contritely and with a humble spirit.[12]
To summarize, this story illustrates that the Talmudic argument
rests on the following principles:
(a) the independence of human reason in matters of law.
(b) the principle of majority rule.

---

[12] See Y.I. Halevy, *Dorot Ha-Rishonim*, (1987) where the character of R. Eliezer
is analyzed in great detail. Halevy (Dorot I, 5, 374ff) defends him, whereas Weiss
(Dorot II, p. 81) criticizes him.

A Sugya: The Notion of Probability

In Talmudic dialectics the principle of majority rule is associated closely with questions of probability. The strength of that association is underlined by the fact that the term for probability is *Rubba*, which is the Aramaic counterpart of the Hebrew noun, ROV, meaning "majority". Hence, as one further illustration of the talmudic methodology it is appropriate to consider the rabbi's employment of the principle of probability. This latter constitutes one side of a coin for which the principle of majority rule provides the other. The following *Sugya* probes their relationship.[13] Our analysis is based on Talmud. *Hulin* (pp. 11a–12a), and on an outstanding, recent study of Louis Jacobs.[14]

To establish the ground of debate, this *Sugya* opens with a question:

> "Where do we derive the rule laid down by the Rabbis that we are guided by the principle of probability (*rubba*)?"

The response to this query is one of surprise: "how?". Scripture, it is observed, clearly states: "Turn after the majority" (Ex. 23:2). Here, the reference is to a verse in the *Book of Exodus* which reads (Revised Standard Version): "You shall not follow a multitude to do evil; nor shall you bear witness in a suit, turning aside after a multitude, so as to pervert justice." The talmudic scholars interpreted the first part of the verse as indicating that the majority *should be followed* except in the case of "following to do evil".

The debate proceeds by way of a rejoinder to the foregoing. This rejoinder can be paraphrased, as follows:

Granted that in certain instances we apply the principle of *rubba*. For example, in the case of a capital charge before the Lower Sanhedrin where twelve judges declare the accused innocent and eleven declare him guilty, the principle of *rubba* is followed because a definite majority is "before us." So too, in the case of "nine vendors" with ritually clean meat and one unclean, where a chunk (of meat) was found on the street, we assume that it has "separated from the majority", for the very same reason. But, what if the majority is *not* "before us", as in the case of a levirate marriage of a boy or girl under age?

---

[13] A *sugya* is an aggregate of diverse issues used in a Talmudic discourse, augmented by an array of pro's and con's, contradictions and refutations, give and take, etc., for the purpose of hammering out a normative principle or a cardinal rule.

[14] Louis Jacobs, *The Talmudic Argument* (Cambridge: University Press, 1984). See especially, the section *Rubba* (pp. 50–63).

Here, the debater is referring to the *Book of Deuteronomy*, 25:5–10 which enjoins that if a man dies childless, his surviving brother should marry his widow for the explicit purpose of raising an heir in the dead brother's name. Ordinarily, such a marriage is forbidden, a prohibition which clearly implies that if either the levir or the widow is sterile, they should not marry each other.

The problem in the case of a levirate marriage of a boy or a girl under age is that it is impossible to ascertain whether or not either one is fertile. In this case, the majority is not "before us". Hence, how does one follow the principle of probability, understood as "turning after the majority", in this instance?

This point is well taken, since the subject of levirate marriage of those under age is a disputed one (*Yebamot*, 61b). Rabbi Meir is against such a marriage because it may turn out that either one may be sterile. On the other hand, the Sages approve of the marriage on the ground that most minors turn out to be fertile. These eminent authorities, then, accept the principle of *Rubba* even though the majority is not "before us".

The debate does not end at this stage. Rather, it has just begun. The battleground is now ready, the forces are arranged, and the *Amoraim*, like skillful chess-players are poised to engage their brilliant strategies. Each tries his hand on the talmudic chess board in order to prove his point and to settle the question. Ten attempts are made, and ten proofs are offered. Some of these are refuted, whilst others stand. The upshot is that, although the principle of *rubba* is generally followed, it is applied only with certain qualifications to levirate marriage of the underaged.

An Exception

The foregoing section illustrates something of the character of Taludic controversy. It is further illustrative of that character to remark that, despite the emphasis on the rule of the majority, an exception is allowed in one important area. The rabbis are not given to adhere slavishly to general principles when these do not appear to serve the cause of justice in society.

The rule of the majority is not followed in monetary matters. Hence, in pecuniary disputes the probability principle is not applied. Rather, the claimant in any such case must present satisfactory evidence and thereby, prove his claim in a court of law.[15] The

---

[15] See, *B.K.* 27b, 46 a-b; *Hulin* 10b; *Yeb.* 31a. See also, *Tossafot B.K.* 27b.

reason for this exception is that the defendant is allowed to possess two attributes which tell in his favour. The first of these attributes is a "minority" status. The second is the status of having a "presumption".

An example of the talmudic reasoning in this regard is the case where the defendant sold an ox to the claimant, and the ox was found to be a gorer. The claimant now wants his money back on the ground that his purchase was a "mistaken transaction". Most people, it can be allowed, acquire an ox for purposes of ploughing, and a gorer is not satisfactory for that purpose. Yet, this does not necessarily put the defendant in the wrong. He can claim "minority" status in that he can contend that he sold the ox for consumption as meat. Secondly, the defendant is given the "presumption" of being the owner of the money in question. When the status of "minority" and the status of "presumption" are combined, these are held to constitute a counterbalance to the principle of *Rubba*. If the claimant is to have his money, he must present sufficient evidence in court. The onus of proof is on the claimant, despite the fact that the majority of persons purchase oxen for ploughing.

In conclusion, it should be remarked also that a range of special circumstances may justify departure from the principle of majority rule. As Menachem Elon, an Israeli Supreme Court Justice, writes:

"Concepts such as 'darkhei shalom' (ways of peace), 'tikun olam' (reforming the world), 'pekuakh nefesh' (saving an endangered life) and 'sheat hadechak' (in time of an emergency) are extra spirit ('neshama yetera') of the world of halakha. They are an integral part of the Law."[16]

Given such circumstances, it is not impossible that a decision is based on a minority.

Endnote

The purpose of this chapter has been to provide an outline of the intellectual setting for economic analysis in the Talmud, with reference to the formation of the work and its methodology. However, it is an outline only, and some readers may wish to enquire further concerning that setting. For those readers, the following full-length studies are strongly recommended:

---

[16] Etta Bick (ed.), *Judaic Sources of Human Rights* (Tel Aviv: Israel Diaspora Institute, Tel Aviv University, 1989), p. 11.

David Weiss-Halivni, *Midrash, Mishna and Gemara* (Harvard: Harvard University Press, 1986); Moses Mielziner, *Introduction to the Talmud* (New York: Block, 1967); George Horowitz, *The Spirit of Jewish Law* (New York: Central Book Company, 1953); Hermann L. Strack, *Introduction to the Talmud and Midrash* (New York: Harper and Row, 1920). Dov Zlotnick, *The Iron Pillar-Mishnah, Reduction, Form and Intent*, (KTAV Publishing House, Inc., 1988)

CHAPTER TWO
OLD WISDOM AND THE WRITTEN LAW

In the foregoing chapter, we demonstrated that Talmudic argument rests on the principle of majority rule, and on the affirmation of the independence of human reason in matters of law. This latter affirmation has strong biblical roots which are grounded in the Wisdom tradition of early Jewish literature, and in the concern of the ancients to establish objective codes governing social conduct. Wisdom emphasized the role of intellectual endeavour in arriving at the truth of a matter. Law established the goals towards which those professing wisdom should direct their attentions.

It is in the contexts of Wisdom and the Law that the biblical backgrounds to the major thrusts of Talmudic economic analysis can be best appreciated. The Talmudic scholars went well beyond their biblical predecessors, in terms of analytical refinement, on a number of points, especially as they were obliged to deal with economic relationships of increasing complexity. Some of the processes of refinement are detailed in the chapters which follow. Nevertheless, the talmudists remained true to the biblical insights on economic life which struck them as relevant. Certain of those insights became major points of departure for talmudic economic analysis.

The purpose of this chapter is to outline the scope and limitations of economic analysis in biblical Wisdom literature, with special reference to the older sections of the *Book of Proverbs*. Secondly, the chapter surveys the economic content of the wide-ranging legal codes upon which the non-oral elements of the talmudic tradition are based.

Old Wisdom

It is generally recognized now that at some point (which might be as early as the reign of Hezekiah, 714–686 B.C.E.) the wisdom tradition among the Hebrews experienced a significant reorientation. Before the change, Wisdom,

> concerned itself with norms of individual behaviour conducive to a good and satisfying life for that person, and to the community well-being . . . This kind of wisdom was mundane, empirical, practical,

and prudential in subject matter and tone. Its sanctions were chiefly those of success and social approval.[1]

Although acknowledgement of a divine order shaping the affairs of mankind is an essential feature of literature in this vein, much of its emphasis is secular, utilitarian and humanistic. There is a good deal of common ground between Old Wisdom and the post-metaphysical tradition of modern Western thought in which Economics has attained the status of a distinct discipline.[2]

New Wisdom offers a considerable contrast. With regard to the contrast, von Rad writes that,

> ... there appears what can almost be called a counter-movement. More specialised, theological questions had arisen, and later wisdom saw itself faced with the task, without sacrificing to the secularity of creation the knowledge that had been acquired, the task of bringing the world and man back once again into the centre of God's sphere of activity.[3]

Wisdom, in this new guise, is not simply the manifestation of a human activity. All wisdom is from God, as is the Torah.

As the counter-movement developed, instruction in Wisdom and the Law were brought together. "The Torah", observes Johannes Lindblom, "was then regarded as the epitome of all Wisdom and the standard of Wisdom; and the teaching in the Wisdom schools manifestly also included instruction in the principles and commands of the law."[4] Eventually, wisdom came to be identified with Torah, an identification which, as Moshe Weinfeld remarks, meant that, "both were conceived together as a heavenly element which descended from heaven to take its abode among the children of Israel (Ben-Sira, 24)."[5]

The origins and time of entry of Old Wisdom in Israel are matters of some contention. One widely accepted view associates these with the reign of Solomon (960–931 B.C.E.). The sources, it is claimed, are Egyptian in the main, and the foundation of a local

---

[1] R.B.Y. Scott, *The Way of Wisdom in the Old Testament*, (N.Y.: Macmillan, 1971), pp. 137–8.
[2] C.F., E.W. Heaton, *Solomon's New Men* (London: Thames and Hudson, 1974), p. 140.
[3] G. von Rad, *Wisdom in Israel* (London: S.C.M., 1972), p. 317.
[4] J. Lindblom, "Wisdom in the Old Testament Prophets", in, M. Noth and D. Winton Thomas (eds.), *Wisdom in Israel and in the Ancient Near East* (Leiden: Brill, 1969), p. 196.
[5] M. Weinfeld, *Deuteronomy and the Deuteronomic School* (Oxford: Clarendon, 1972), p. 256.

tradition was bound up with the need for formal schooling of civil servants on the Egyptian model. William McKane, for example, states:

> It is a reasonable assumption that the Instruction was appropriated by Israel as early as the reign of Solomon, when a class of officials came into existence to serve the new structure of the state, and when there was a consequent need for Instruction with the same educational function as it had in Egypt. There it was located in schools where an elite was trained for the service of the state; likewise, when Solomon created a civil service (perhaps on the Egyptian model) there would have been a demand for a similar type of school and for such an instrument of vocational education.[6]

Despite the strong grounds for this view, some writers contest one or more of the propositions it affirms. R.N. Whybray, for example, believes that Israelite wisdom literature is not so much a court phenomenon as one which is a predominantly native development with roots in the nomadic or semi-nomadic period of the nation's formation. In addition, it does not stem from the endeavours of a distinct class of "wise men" whose profession was that of instructing civil servants. Rather, "it was written for an adult educated class not confined to court circles, for their instruction and entertainment, by some of the more gifted members of that class whom their contemporaries and successors honoured with the epithet *hakam*."[7]

In favour of Whybray's demur, it can be observed that from an economist's viewpoint, Old Wisdom is of interest because of its regard for micro-economic analysis. It is almost totally innocent of macro-economic propositions, yet one might have expected that if this literature was intended for the instruction of those who were to occupy the corridors of power in central government there would have been a proportion of dictums of a macro-economic nature, i.e., comments designed to draw the attention of the decision-making elite to functional relationships between aggregate variables. There is little in the *Books of Proverbs*, for example, which can compare with the macro orientation of the detailing of Joseph's agrarian policy in the *Book of Genesis* (Gen. 47:13–26). *Proverbs* 14:28 pro-

---

[6] W. McKane, *Proverbs, a New Approach* (London: S.C.M., 1970), pp. 8–9. See also, E.W. Heaton, op. cit., p. 130. A New Testament text which might be cited in support of a Jewish belief in an Egyptian origin for the Israelite wisdom tradition is, Acts 7:22. The text states: "So Moses was taught all the wisdom of the Egyptians and became a man with power both in his speech and his actions."

[7] R.N. Whybray, *The Intellectual Tradition in the Old Testament* (Berlin and New York: de Gruyter, 1974), pp. 60–61.

poses a functional relationship between total size of population and the status of the ruler concerned, but otherwise, the Book offers scant guidance on aggregates for the national policy adviser.

Proverbs and Economic Analysis

Whatever the point of entry or the intended audience of Old Wisdom, it is clear that its exponents were involved in economic analysis at the micro level. This is not to say that in their conceptions, Economics as a discipline attained distinct status as a branch of the division of intellectual labour. Almost certainly, it did not. Nevertheless, it is striking that a number of the analytical propositions common to modern Economics textbooks echo the insights of the wise men.

On the topic of exchange relationships, a widely-read, modern textbook states:

> In economic transactions, one party does not lose what the other gains . . . The money the buyer parts with is necessarily identical with the money the seller receives. But the *welfare* significance of the good to the buyer is not identical to the money he parts with. In terms of utility, he enjoys a 'consumer's surplus'.[8]

The existence of such a surplus for the buyer is identified also by the ancient writers. They observe (in the context of the ritual haggling associated with Eastern market exchange): "'A bad, bad bargain!', says a buyer, but as he makes off he congratulates himself." (Pr. 20:14).[9]

With respect to consumer behaviour, another modern textbook relates: "The wants that can be satisfied by consuming goods and services may be regarded, for all practical purposes in today's world, as insatiable."[10] Not only in "today's world", but, if the wise men are correct, this generalization was true in ancient times. They remark: "Sheol and Abaddon are insatiable, a man's eyes are never satisfied." (Pr. 27:20). Further, like the modern economist, the ancients perceive that although it may be valid to posit the insatiability of wants in general, particular wants are satiable. The

---

[8] P. Samuelson, K. Hancock and R. Wallace, *Economics* (Sydney: McGraw Hill, 1975), p. 490.

[9] Unless indicated otherwise, the translations of quotations from *Proverbs* are those of W. McKane, op. cit. In addition, the same writer's classification of particular proverbs is followed with respect to their exemplifying either old or new wisdom.

[10] R.G. Lipsey, *An Introduction to Positive Economics* (London: Weidenfeld and Nicolson, 1979), p. 53.

compilers of *Proverbs* are no strangers to the Law of Diminishing
Utility, which, they hold, applies even in the case where a whole-
some delicacy like honey is the consumption item in question: "If
you find honey, eat what suffices you, lest you have surfeit of it and
vomit it up." (Pr. 25:16). "The person who is satiated tramples on
honey, but everything bitter is sweet to the one who is hungry."
(Pr. 27:7).

This second sentence is of particular interest in that it indicates
that the sages were quite aware that economic behaviour has two
limits. Calculating, allocative activity becomes irrelevant not only
at extremes of abundance but also at the extremes of dearth.[11]

Further generalizations in Old Wisdom concerning economic
behaviour relate, for the most part, to the acquisition of wealth by
the individual. These generalizations are made from the standpoint that it is a good thing for the individual to be wealthy,
provided he is capable to coping with the situation. The writers
warn against any personal obsession with gaining wealth or with
retaining it, especially as the gaining may be personally debilitating
and the retention extremely demanding (Pr. 23:4–5). Nevertheless,
they affirm that, "a rich man's wealth is his strong city, but the
poverty of the poor is disaster for them." (Pr. 10:15). Again, they
declare: "The crown of wise men is their wealth, but the wreath of
fools is folly." (Pr. 14:24). This last statement is especially indicative of the attitude of the earlier wisdom writers, and William
McKane comments:

> The sentence means that wealth is a fitting adornment of wisdom and
> is an aspect of the general recognition of his worth to which a wise
> man is entitled. His wealth is not an extraneous factor nor an alien
> intrusion, but is a confirmation of his intrinsic merit as a sage and the
> position of commanding influence which he has attained. It is there-
> fore associated with the climax of his career and in this sense is the
> crown of his efforts.[12]

The same understanding of a link between Wealth and Wisdom
is expressed in dramatic form in the *Book of Kings*. There, the
personal wealth of the archetypal wisdom figure, Solomon, as well
as the prosperity of the kingdom during his reign, are explained as
gifts of God associated with the granting of Solomon's request for
the gift of wisdom. Wealth is *added* as an adornment for the wise. It

---

[11] This same insight concerning dearth and the irrelevance of economic calculation is offered by the Greek poet, Hesiod (c. 750 B.C.E.). On Hesiod, see, B.
Gordon, *Economic Analysis Before Adam Smith* (London: Macmillan, 1975), p. 5.

[12] W. McKane, op. cit., p. 466.

is a *by-product* of a fulfilled desire to attain discernment, as the dialogue between Solomon and God illustrates (1 Kings 3:9–13).

The Acquisition of Wealth

Given the association of Wealth and Wisdom, it is understandable that the *Book of Proverbs* pays attention to the factors involved in the attainment of riches. The factor which is emphasized most frequently is diligence, i.e. steady application and perseverance. There are numerous sentences to this effect, e.g., "Half-hearted effort makes for poverty, but diligence makes for wealth." (Pr. 10:4). Again, only "a little folding of the hands" is likely to give rise to the onset of poverty and beggary (Pr. 24:30–34).[13]

Beyond diligence, there is the factor of investment. In this respect, the wise men counsel caution. They observe that, "wealth gained speculatively dwindles", and that, "all who are in a hurry produce nothing but scarcity." (Pr. 13:11; 21:5). They cannot support an eager thrust with a view to quick profit. Yet, at the same time, they cannot abide the individual who does not employ accumulated wealth: "Do not eat with a miser, nor let your appetite be whetted by his tit-bits, for he is like a hair in the throat." (Pr. 23:6–7). Rejecting these extremes of feverish speculation and dogged hoarding, Old Wisdom seems to recommend that those persons who have the resources should undertake a broad range of expenditures beyond those required by their personal or household needs. Whether or not all or any of these outlays ought to be geared to the expectation of profit is not clear. Yet, it is observed, such as course will result in the accumulation of capital. In addition, the enlightened self-interest of those who adopt this course will prove to be to the advantage of society as a whole. The relevant passage reads: "There is the man who disburses his wealth freely and yet is always getting richer, there is another whose miserliness leads only to want. He who creates prosperity is himself prosperous, and he who satisfies others is himself satisfied." (Pr. 11:24–25).

Taken together, the foregoing sentences suggest that the contributors of the earlier material in Proverbs recognized the relationship between investment and the attainment of wealth, but they lacked the degree of personal involvement in "high finance" which might have enabled them to be more specific about that relationship. This lack is not surprising if, as E.W. Heaton con-

---

[13] See also, Pr. 12:24; 12:27; 13:4; 18:9; 20:13; 21:25.

tends, "the man of Proverbs is a highly-motivated member of the lower middle class."[14]

Apart from diligence and sober engagement in expenditure beyond that required for personal consumption, Old Wisdom counsels attention to the technical problem of achieving optimal combinations of factor inputs in production. A production function, it is realized, is subject to the law of variable proportions, and hence, it is observed: "Where there are no oxen, there is a crib of grain, but crops are increased by the strength of an ox." (Pr. 14:4).

The significance of this sentence has been remarked by William McKane, who writes that,

> draught animals are an indispensible asset for a farmer and that without them his labour is unproductive . . . The balance between the grain which the oxen consume and their productive capacity has to be ascertained. They are a kind of capital equipment which has to be used economically; it is important not to have too few or too many, but to employ the number which secures maximum production at the lowest costs.[15]

A further factor in the acquisition and proper management of wealth is the avoidance of involvement in business deals which entail credit arrangements. The wise man will shun the role of debtor, since, "A borrower is a slave to the man who lends." (Pr. 22:7). He will also be extremely cautious about becoming a "sleeping partner" who is personally liable: "Do not make a habit of striking hands, of going surety for debts. If you have no resources to settle them, why should your bed be taken from under you!" (Pr. 22:26–27).

The risk of loss of capital ("your bed") is seen as being particularly high in deals which involve outsiders: "Take his garment [capital] for he has gone surety for a stranger; secure yourself against him, for his is liable for foreigners." (Pr. 27:13; see also, 20:16). The best course, it would appear, is to follow the path of individualistic, capitalist endeavour. "He who hates contracts", it is claimed, "will be secure." (Pr. 11:15). It is unwise to extend one's legal responsibilities beyond the circle of family and/or friends of long-standing.

---

[14] E.W. Heaton, op. cit., p. 124.
[15] W. McKane, op. cit., p. 471.

The Legal Codes

A compilation such as the *Book of Proverbs* illustrates something of the range of analytical insights concerning economic behaviour with which the founders of the Talmudic tradition were thoroughly familiar. However, of even greater importance for the direction of economic enquiry in the Talmud are the prescriptions of the law codes of the Pentateuch. Those codes include a close concern with the detail of the day-to-day conduct of economic relationships, and they are most comprehensive in this regard.

In the *Book of Exodus*, the main collections of law are the Decalogue (Ex. 20:1–17), the Code of the Covenant (Ex. 20:22–23:33), and the Code of the Renewal of the Covenant (Ex. 34:10–26). There is a restatement of the Decalogue in the *Book of Deuteronomy* (Dt. 5:6–21), and the same Book provides an extensive set of regulations known as the Deuteronomic Code (Dt. 12:1–26:15). Leviticus adds the Holiness Code (Lv. 17–26) plus an appendix which deals with dedicatory gifts (Lv. 27:1–34). Within these bodies of law there are extensive examinations of the use of free labour, arable land, real capital, and money. In addition, the codes address issues of economic welfare, consumption patterns, and valuation.

The Use of Free Labour

As with the *Book of Genesis*, the law codes affirm that work is a divine ordinance for man. In the priestly version of the Decalogue, for example, God commands: "For six days you shall labour and do all your work" (Ex. 20:9). The same prescription is given in Deuteronomy 5:13 (c.f., Ex. 34:21, and Lv. 23:3). No attempt is made to specify a list of, or to rank, legitimate occupations, but one type which is expressly, and repeatedly, forbidden is the fashioning of graven images whether in metal, wood or stone.[16]

A general, and quite fundamental, restriction on the application of labour is the command to rest on the sabbath day. This edict is not for free adult male Israelites alone, but it extends to their dependents and even their work animals: "The seventh day is a sabbath for Yahweh your God. You shall do no work on that day, neither you nor your son your daughter nor your servants, men or

---

[16] Ex. 20:4, 23; 34:17; Dt. 5:8; Lv. 19:4; 26:1. For discussion of the prohibition see, Anthony Phillips, *Ancient Israel's Criminal Law: a New Approach to the Decalogue*, (Oxford: Blackwell, 1970), pp. 48–52.

women, nor your animals nor the stranger who lives with you."
(Ex. 20:10).

The *Book of Exodus* offers two kinds of rationale for this containment of productive activity. One kind looks toward the God-man
element in the covenant relationship. The reasoning is: "For in six
days Yahweh made the heavens and the earth and the sea and all
that these hold, but on the seventh day he rested; that is why
Yahweh has blessed the sabbath day and made it sacred." (Ex.
20:11). The other kind refers to the man-man aspect of covenant
obligation: "for six days you shall do your work, but stop on the
seventh day, so that your ox and your donkey may rest and the son
of your slave girl have a breathing space, and the stranger too."
(Ex. 23:12). Deuteronomy 5:14 also suggests this second, humanistic rationale. However, it continues: "Remember that you were a
servant in the land of Egypt, and that Yahweh your God brought
you out from there with mighty hand and outstretched arm; because of this, Yahweh your God has commanded you to keep the
sabbath day." (Dt. 5:15). Here, an historical occurrence has replaced a sacral one (God's resting) as the explanation.[17] Despite the
variations, these texts convey a common message: for men who live
with God, work is not to constitute the whole of their existence.
Work maybe a divine ordinance, but it does not exhaust the meaning of life.

The Use of Arable Land

The principle of six periods of work followed by one period of rest is
carried over to condition the manner in which the Israelites are to
use the soil of the Land which God has given them. They are to
allow it to lie fallow for one year in every seven. The Book of the
Covenant states: "For six years you may sow your land and gather
its produce, but in the seventh year you must let it lie fallow and
forego all produce from it. Those of your people who are poor may
take food from it, and let the wild animals feed on what they leave.
You shall do the same with your vineyard and your olive grove."
(Ex. 23:10–11).

It might be inferred that, given the references to "the poor" and
"the wild animals", an amalgam of humanitarian and ecological
considerations underlies this statute. However, it must be allowed
that this law could have been promulgated as a form of required

---

[17] Reasons for the shifting emphases are considered in Anthony Phillips, op.
cit., pp. 66–73.

response to the God-man relationship of the covenant. Alternately, it may even represent an adoption of a Canaanite custom long established in the region. The origins of the sabbatical year remain matters for wide-ranging speculation.

While Deuteronomy considers the question of the seventh year, it makes no reference to the land (Dt. 15:1–18). Here, the emphasis is on remission of debts and the release of debt slaves. By contrast, the Holiness Code reaffirms the principle of a fallow. Nature, as well as man and his animals, is to observe God's law. The Code declares that, "the land is to keep a sabbath's rest for Yahweh . . . It is to be a year of rest for the land." (Lv. 25:1–7). Leviticus proceeds even further. It extends the general numerical principle associated with work and rest to proclaim the necessity of a "fiftieth year", the Year of Jubilee. In that year, "you will not sow, you will not harvest the ungathered corn, you will not gather from the untrimmed vine. The jubilee is to be a holy thing to you, you will eat what comes from the fields." (Lv. 25:11–12). An additional provision of jubilee is the return of possession of argicultural land to the descendants of the family which had been allocated that land in the original expropriation of Canaan (Lv. 25:23–28). A member of another family who has purchased the right to the use of that land is obliged to give it up.[18]

Underlying both jubilee and sabbatical is the conviction that the Land belongs to God. He is its true owner. The Land's "resting" is an acknowledgement of this ownership, as is the proposed periodic return to the original occupying family. Whether or not the sabbatical laws, let alone those of jubilee, were ever observed, and in what form and in which periods, are the subjects of considerable debate. Did the laws have a practical character, at least in simple rural economies? Were they applied at fixed time intervals throughout Israel, or rather, invoked in a piecemeal fashion as the duration of individual contracts of sale dictated? Whatever the answers which emerge, however, it is clear that for some of the law givers, land as a factor of production was a vital part of the covenant relationship. The soil of Canaan was the free gift of God to his chosen ones. No man-made arrangements concerning its use could be permitted to obscure that reality.[19] It is indicative that,

---

[18] Leviticus 25 also provides for the redemption of land outside jubilee. Either the original vendor, or a relative of his, has the right to buy back family land which has been sold to an outsider. For detail, consult, Raymond Westbrook, "Redemption of Land", *Israel Law Review*, Vol. 6 (1971), pp. 367–375.

[19] C.f. Walter Brueggemann, *The Land: Place as Gift, Promise, and Challenge in Biblical Faith* (Philadelphia: Fortress, 1977), p. 60.

according to traditional teaching, the year of Jubilee was begun with the blowing of the ram's horn on Yom Kippur. This practice is symbolic of the need for cleansing and purification. The ensuing period was to be a time of spiritual renewal which necessarily involved reformation of existing economic relationships. The legislators refused to divorce the spiritual and the economic.

The Use of Real Capital

In the economies of antiquity, slaves were crucial elements in the structure of private and public capital. This was the case in the Israel of the kings, but the Jewish legislators sought to contain this feature of the economy within strict bounds. The freedom of the owners of this type of capital to use it as they wished was far from absolute. This was especially so where Hebrews had been forced into slavery because of debt.

The Book of the Covenant contains a number of specific provisions to protect both male and female slaves (see especially, Ex. 21:1–27). If, for example, a slave loses an eye or a tooth because of a blow from his master, the slave is to be set free. Again, a female slave cannot be sold to a foreigner, and she retains her conjugal rights should her master take another wife. All male Hebrew slaves must be released from bondage in their seventh year of service, should the slave desire such release. This latter law, according to Anthony Phillips, represents the secularization of an earlier custom which, "provided for the release of Hebrew male slaves at the end of every seventh year in order that they might be able to take part in the covenant renewal festival".[20] The fact that the slave might forego the opportunity for freedom also points to a circumstance of pre-monarchical Israel. Robert North writes: "Whereas in a democratic society the loss of liberty is an unmixed evil, in an unpoliced tribal society it was far less than the evil of being free."[21]

Release after six years of service is a provision which is taken up and developed in the Deuteronomic Code (Dt. 15:12–18). Here, the departing slave is to be given, "a generous provision from your flock, your threshing-floor, your winepress." Freedom is to be granted women as well as men. The master, who may be regretting the loss of these useful factor inputs, is consoled with the economic-

---

[20] A. Phillips, op. cit., p. 74.
[21] R. North, *Sociology of the Biblical Jubilee* (Rome: Pontifical Biblical Institute, 1954), p. 142. This grim reality is usually neglected by the proponents of romantic notions concerning conditions of life before the monarchy.

rational consideration that he has been getting cheap labour over the recent past. A slave, it is affirmed, "is worth twice the cost of a hired servant and has served you for six years."[22] Another consideration invokes the God-man dimensions of the covenant. The law of release was anticipated by the liberating action of God himself: "Remember that you were a slave in the land of Egypt and that Yahweh your God redeemed you; that is why I lay this charge on you today."

It is a prior action of God then which gives this law its fundamental rationale. God has shown himself to be a releaser of Hebrew slaves. Those who understand themselves as the People of God cannot readily act in a contradictory fashion. Rather, they must imitate their Lord.

There is some contrast at this point between Deuteronomy and the legislation from the priestly source. In Leviticus there is no mention of the release of individual slaves after they served for six years. All Hebrew debt-slaves are to be set free during Jubilee with their families, and their ancestral property is to be restored to them. In the interim, each of them is to be treated, "like a hired man or a guest." (Lv. 25:39–42). No analogous considerations are to be shown non-Hebrew human capital. This latter, "shall be your property and you may leave them as an inheritance to your sons after you, to hold in perpetual possession. These you may have for slaves; but to your brothers, the sons of Israel, you must not be hard masters." (Lv. 25:45–46). The sons of Israel have been taken from the service of Pharoah in Egypt and have been dedicated to the service of God. (Lv. 25:42). The action of God has placed them in a special category which requires a care that no other action of God has indicated as appropriate for foreigners.[23]

Apart from slaves, there are other types of capital, animate and inanimate, upon which conditions of use are placed. It is forbidden to sow two kinds of seed in the one field, or to plough with an ass and an ox harnessed together, or to allow different strains of cattle to interbreed (Dt. 22:9–10; Lv. 19:19). The owners of oxen face substantial penalties for failure to protect persons and property from the beasts (Ex. 21:28–36). These same animals must not be muzzled when they are treading out grain (Dt. 25:4).

---

[22] Concerning this observation, see, Yair Zakovitch, "Some Remnants of Ancient Laws in the Deuteronomic Code", *Israel Law Review*, Vol. 9 (1974), pp. 349–351.

[23] The bases of the non-cosmopolitan nature of early Jewish social thought are explored in, Harry M. Orlinsky, "Who is the Ideal Jew: the Biblical View", *Judaism*, Vol. 13 (1964), pp. 19–28.

Trees are of concern to the law givers. Newly planted fruit trees must be allowed to mature for five years before their produce is systematically harvested (Lv. 19:23–25). In Deuteronomy, one of the laws of warfare forbids the destruction of fruit trees in aid of the seige of a town (Dt. 20:19–20). Here, the reader is asked: "Is the tree in the fields human that you should besiege it too?" This particular edict, together with those on the treatment of oxen and of birds (Dt. 25:4; 26:6–7), are seen by some commentators as demonstrating that Israel's covenant with God involved definite obligations concerning Nature. Eugene Maly, for example, writes: "Respect for nature, therefore, whether it be in the form of oxen, birds or trees, is not simply a humanitarian gesture. It is part of the divine imperative that determines Israel's ultimate destiny."[24]

The Use of Money

There is no doubt that the law givers view money as a useful social institution. This is evident even in the earlier codes which go so far as to positively require payments in money rather than in goods, in some instances. For example, the Code of the Covenant states: "When a man leaves a pit uncovered, or when he digs one but does not cover it, should an ox, or donkey fall into it, then the owner of the pit shall make up for the loss: he must pay its owner money, and the dead animal shall be his own." (Ex. 21:33–34). Another instance of a requirement to meet damages with a sum of money is Ex. 22:16–17.

Further, the later codes employ money as a means of enhancing the nation's service to the Lord. Deuteronomy, for example, promotes monetisation in aid of cultic observance. That observance obliges the Israelites to bring a tithe of their produce, in kind, as an annual offering to God, "in the place he chooses to give his name a home." However, the obligation to tithe in kind is not absolute: "If the road is too long for you, if you cannot bring your tithe because the place in which Yahweh chooses to make a home for his name is too far, when Yahweh your God has blessed you, you must turn your tithe into money, and with the money clasped in your hand you must go to the place chosen by Yahweh; there you may spend the money on whatever you like, oxen, sheep, wine, strong drink, anything your heart desires." (Dr. 14:24–26). The transformation

---

[24] E.H. Maly, "Man and Nature in the Old Testament", *Studia Missionalia*, 19 (1970), p. 313. On the significance of Dt. 20:19–20, see also, G. von Rad, *Deuteronomy, a Commentary* (London: S.C.M., 1976), p. 133.

in thought which this concession represents has been remarked by Gerhard von Rad. He writes: "From the standpoint of old conceptions of a sacrifice this is an astonishing rationalization of cultic usage."[25]

Rationalization of usage is also a feature of Leviticus. The Holiness Code requires the priests of the sanctuary to be extraordinarily adept at handling the intricacies of a money economy if they are to ensure fulfilment by Israel of its covenant obligations. In the twenty-seventh chapter of Leviticus, God gives Moses on Mount Sinai a list of detailed instructions on how sanctuary tariffs and estimates are to be calculated in terms of silver shekels. The contents of this chapter are indicative of the thoroughgoing integration of the life of the Temple with the system of economic exchanges throughout the nation.

The major respect in which the use of money is restricted is in the sphere of lending. It is not clear just how far the restrictions are intended to extend. However, there are certain circumstances in which it is forbidden to use money for the purpose of earning interest on a loan. The Code of Covenant, for example, states that interest must not be taken on loans to the poor (Ex. 22:25–26). Deuteronomy might be interpreted as going further than this in prohibiting interest-taking on any loan from one Israelite to another (Dt. 23:20–21). On the other hand, Leviticus 25:35–37 could be understood to allow for interest in the case of commercial loans or of loans to the well-to-do. Probably, there was not a complete ban on interest in lending among Israelites, but the scope for the legitimate use of money in that respect cannot be established with precision.[26]

Economic Welfare

The Codes of the Pentateuch do not confine themselves merely to the containment of the use of the factors of production. The fruits of the employment of those factors must be distributed, consumed, and exchanged in accord with the dictates of the covenant which ensures Israel's identity. God did not go to the trouble of redeeming the Nation so that, in its turn, it could set up a social order as harsh and inhumane as the one from which it was delivered. God's

---

[25] G. Von Rad, op. cit., p. 103.
[26] For more extensive discussion consult, B. Gordon, "Lending at Interest: Some Jewish, Greek and Christian Approaches, 800 B.C.–A.D. 100," *History of Political Economy*, 14 (1982), pp. 406–426.

chosen people are to reflect in their daily communal interchanges that same pattern of care and consideration which he has shown. They are an elevated and priestly people which is obliged to act with the combination of compassion and rationality that acceptance of such status demands.

Widows, orphans, strangers, and the Levites made destitute by the cultic centralization of the Deuteronomic reform are accorded special attention.[27] Hence, the Code of the Covenant counsels care for such disadvantaged persons (Ex. 22:21–24; 23:9). Deuteronomy is much more specific regarding welfare provisions. This code requires that the poor are enabled to participate in the feasting associated with certain annual festivals (Dt. 16:10–14). Further, in every third year, the poor have the right to a tithe of the harvests (Dt. 14:28–29; 26:12–13).[28] They also have gleaning rights in any harvest period. Deuteronomy states: "When reaping the harvest in your field, if you have overlooked a sheaf in that field, do not go back for it. Leave it for the stranger, the orphan and the widow, so that Yahweh your God may bless you in all your undertakings. When you beat your olive trees you must not go over the branches twice. Let anything left be for the stranger, the orphan and the widow. When you harvest your vineyard you must not pick it over a second time. Let anything left be for the stranger, the orphan and the widow." (Dt. 24:19–21).

This passage on gleaning rights affords a vivid illustration of the combination of rationality and compassion which informed the development of Jewish welfare legislation. Perhaps, the custom of leaving a portion of a crop in a field was intended originally as a means of propitiating the fertility spirits of the soil by allocating them a share in the crop. Here, the ancient custom is retained, but it is demythologized and humanized. The principle of gleaning rights is also affirmed in Leviticus 19:19–20 and 23:22.

Other groups identified as warranting special attention are the poor day-labourers and those who have fallen into debt. Many of

---

[27] Levites who had previously tended shrines in rural areas must have faced particular difficulties. The Levites, according to custom, had "no share or inheritance with Israel; they shall live on the foods offered to Yahweh and on his dues." (Dt. 18:1). On the status of the Levites, their duties and their dues, consult the Book of Numbers. (Nb. 3; 4; 8:5–26; 18:1–32; and, 35:1–8).

[28] The tithe was a levy in support of the maintenance of the sanctuary and to provide for participation in sacrificial meals there. Now, in every third year, this to be retained for distribution in the area in which it was collected. On the relationship of the triennial tithe and the Temple tithe, see, Yair Zakovitch, "Some Remnants of Ancient Laws in the Deuteronomic Code", *Israel Law Review*, Vol. 9 (1974), pp. 346–349.

the day-labourers led a hand-to-mouth existence, so their employers are instructed to pay them each day before sundown (Dt. 24:14–15; Lv. 19:13). Relief for debtors is a feature of the sabbatical year. Every seventh year, all claims in respect of debt are to be remitted (Dt. 15:3–4).

Regulation of Consumption

The law-givers of the Pentateuch are not greatly affected by the ascetical considerations which characterise some non-Yahwistic religions. The Nazarite Vow (Num. 6:1–21) seems to represent some concession to asceticism, but in general, the corn and the wine and the oil of the Land are to be accepted as the gifts of God to his people. Should God choose to give these in abundance, his people will not spurn the generosity displayed. However, personal consumption may need to be limited at times with a view to caring for the poor. Further, that consumption is to be regulated in the service of due worship of the Lord of the Covenant. Cultic observance requires the offering of the first fruits of the harvest. (Ex. 22:19; 34:26; Lv. 23:9–21). First-born are "given to God". (Ex. 22:30; 34:19; Dt. 12:17–18; 15:19–22). There are to be tithes of produce (Dt. 14:22–23), which tithes are payments to God as owner of the Land.

A range of dietary practices is prescribed in Dt. 14:3–21, and elsewhere. These extend to abstaining from torn flesh (Ex. 22:31; Lv. 17:15–16) and avoiding the consumption of blood (Dt. 12:16; 12:23–25; 15:23; Lv. 17:10–13; 19:26). Clothing too is a matter for concern. For example, the wearing of garments "woven part of wool, part of linen" is forbidden. (Dt. 22:11; Lv. 19:19). Provisions such as these may represent, in part, the remnants of very ancient taboos. They may also represent, in part, sound common sense for physical well-being in the environs of the ancient Near East.

One member of the community whose habits are singled out for special mention in the Deuteronomic Code is the king. Restrictions are placed on the king's multiplying the possessions at his personal command. He is not to increase the number of his horses or the number of his wives. Further, he must not "increase his gold and silver excessively". (Dt. 17:16–17). In general, his life-style must not be too far removed from that of his fellow countrymen. As von Rad writes:

> Deuteronomy sees in kingship not an office which Yahweh could use for the welfare of his people, but only an institution in which the holder must live in a sphere of extreme peril because he is tempted by

his wealth either to turn away from Yahweh or to lift up his heart above his brethren.[29]

Prices and Values

There is no attempt in the codes to establish a fixed structure of prices for goods and services of every-day trade. Rather, the laws assume the existence of competitive markets in which prices fluctuate freely. The explicit requirement concerning those markets is simply that the persons who deal in them adhere to the practice of using full and just weights, measures and balances. (Dt. 25:13–16; Lv. 19:35–36). In the case of land, the criterion to be used for its valuation is, expected productivity. Land, for the Israelites, is not strictly a sale commodity. God has declared: "Land must not be sold in perpetuity, for the land belongs to me, and to me you are only strangers and guests." (Lv. 25:23). Hence, a member of the covenant community can never actually sell the ancestral land allocated for the use of his family. He can only sell its productive potential, i.e., "a certain number of harvests." (Lv. 25:16). This implies that the purchase price will be a direct function of its expected annual yield and the number of years for which the purchaser is to hold it.

Such a method of valuation emerges explicitly in instructions about land which are consequent on recognition of the custom of Jubilee, the fiftieth year. In that year, the use of each parcel of land is to revert to the descendants of the original, Jewish occupants. Sale and purchase of the use of land must reckon with this custom. Leviticus instructs: "If you buy and sell with your neighbour, let no one wrong his brother. If you buy from your neighbour this must take into account the number of years since jubilee: according to the number of productive years he will fix the price. The greater the number of years, the higher shall be the price demanded; the less the number of years, the greater the reduction; for what he is selling you is a certain number of harvests." (Lv. 25:14–16).[30]

The productivity criterion also appears in the earlier Code of the Covenant when it is considering damages to land. This Code states: "When a man puts his animals out to graze in a field or vineyard and lets his beasts graze in another's field, he must make restitution

---

[29] G. von Rad, op. cit., p. 120. Antipathy to the rule of kings was to continue on over the centuries into Rabbinic Judaism. Consult, David Polish, "Pharisaism and Political Sovereignty", *Judaism*, Vol. 19 (1970), pp. 415–422.

[30] C.f., the arrangements for dedemption of land in Lv. 25:24–28.

for the part of the field that has been grazed in *proportion to its yields.* But if he has let the whole field be grazed, he must make restitution *in proportion to the best crop recorded* in the injured party's field or vineyard." (Ex. 22:4–5).

In the case of slave-capital, the Code of the Covenant is prepared to set the definite sum of thirty shekels as the value of a unit of such capital. (Ex. 21:32). However, there is no attempt to explain how this sum has been established as the appropriate one. The thirty shekels is applied explicitly to both male and female slaves, and there is no mention of age. Rather more revealing is the discussion of redemption of slaves in the Holiness Code. Here, use is made of a going market price as a criterion of evaluation. That price is the wage rate of free labour. The Israelite who wishes to redeem a compatriot from a non-Hebrew owner, "must count the number of years between the year of sale and the jubilee year; the sum of the price of sale must be calculated at the annual rate for these years, his time being valued as that of a hired man." (Lv. 25:50).

Elsewhere in Leviticus there is consideration of values which might be attached to free persons. This occurs in the appendix on dedicatory gifts (Lv. 27:1–34), and here the productivity criterion appears to reemerge. The question is that of the value of a person has been vowed to God but is now to be freed from the obligations of that vow. "Such persons", Martin Noth observes, "were originally set apart for the performance of auxiliary cultic services. Leviticus 27 now clearly provides for release from the fulfilment of such a vow through a money-payment."[31] The size of the money-payment can vary between fifty silver shekels and three. The highest sum is attached to a man aged between twenty and sixty, the lowest sum to a girl aged between one month and five years. (Lv. 27:1–8). Underlying this range there seems to be an assessment of the relative current, annual average productivity of persons in the various categories. In North's opinion: "The essential basis of this assessment lies apparently in the valuation of the person's worth in terms of work at the moment in question."[32]

The appendix on dedicatory gifts is of general interest in that it illustrates the high degree of market knowledge required of the priests of the sanctuary and/or their assistants. To carry out their duties correctly, they need to be extremely well informed on commercial affairs. For example, the priest must be a good judge of the values of a variety of types of livestock and of houses. (Lv. 27:9–15).

---

[31] M. Noth, *Leviticus, a Commentary* (London: S.C.M., 1965), p. 204.
[32] Ibid., p. 205.

Again, he must know the yield of fields in order to apply the productivity criterion: "If a man consecrates one of the fields of his patrimony to Yahweh, its value shall be calculated according to its productivity, at the rate of fifty shekels to one omer of barley." (Lv. 27:16).

This task implies a command of a constant flow of information concerning the relative prices of agricultural commodities. Indeed, it would seem that if some departments of the Temple are to function properly, it must be a major centre for the exchange of economic intelligence. Almost certainly, it could have housed some of the best applied economists in the nation.[33]

---

[33] For analysis of further dimensions of the economics of the Hebrew scriptures, see, B. Gordon, *The Economic Problem in Biblical and Patristic Thought* (Leiden: E.J. Brill, 1989), pp. 1–42.

PART TWO

MACRO-ECONOMIC ISSUES

CHAPTER THREE
ECONOMIC SELF-INTEREST AND SOCIAL PROGRESS

In this chapter we move on from the backgrounds to talmudic economic analysis and begin to consider some of the rabbinic discourses which look forward to much later controversies amongst social theorists. At the outset, it should be emphasized that like other analysts in antiquity and the middle ages, the Talmudic scholars did not set out to establish a systematic body of economic doctrine in the modern sense. Nevertheless, they explored so many of the fundamental issues relating to the operation of free-market economies that, taken together, their insights represent an extremely comprehensive anticipation of European debate in later centuries. Since much of that debate was bound up with the onset of analytical perspectives inspired by an increasing disposition towards economic liberalism, it is appropriate to begin a treatment of the Talmudic anticipations with an investigation of the manner in which the early writers dealt with the role of self-interest in the solution of communal economic problems.

An Ancient Controversy

Talmudic discussion of self-interest and its role was well underway by the second century B.C.E. At this time, *Aggadah*, the non-legal contents of the *Talmud* and *Midrash*, had begun to register the impact of non-Jewish, particularly Greek, concepts.[1] A deal of theological controversy was generated as a result. This controversy was evident within the *Sanhedrin* (or, "council court") which was a prominent institution of the latter part of the Second Temple period.[2] There, as Hellenistic notions gained momentum, the sage, Antigonus of Socho (a leading figure in the "Chamber of Hewn Stones", as it was called) expressed opposition to the inroads of hedonistic philosophy. Antigonus challenged his fellows, as follows:

"Be not like servants who serve their master in order to receive

---

[1] C.f., R.J. Zwi Werblowski and G. Wigoder (eds.), *Encyclopedia of the Jewish Religion* (New York: Holt, Rinehart and Winston, 1965), pp. 15–16.
[2] Consult, *Abot of R. Nathan*, Vol. I, Ch. 5, 13b. On the theological aspects of the controversy, see, Louis Finkelstein, *The Pharisees* (Philadelphia: Jewish Publication Society of America, 1962), Vol. II, pp. 762–79.

wages. Be rather like servants who serve their master without expectation of wages."[3]

The true reward, according to Antigonus, was derived from services rendered out of motives which bore no immediate relationship to self-interest. This was a position which failed to impress a number of his colleagues. Those who remained in the Chamber objected vigorously. The piety of much of the priestly aristocracy was prudential, as was their ethic. These saw no contradiction between moral virtue and a strong personal attachment to the pursuit of individual material gain.

This episode demonstrates that among the eminent scholars there was a substantial division regarding the foundations of legitimate socio-economic behaviour. Antigonus, and like-minded contemporaries, proposed a selfless basis for that behaviour, a basis which they believed was both rational and realistic. Their opponents, on the other hand, espoused an enlightened self-interest. These latter found self-interest to be: the rational mode; a necessary postulate for analysis concerning the behaviour in question; and, no necessary ground for moral condemnation of the individual attached to its maximization. In other words, the opponents of Antigonus took the type of stance which Joseph Schumpeter has described as "a highly sublimated egocentric hedonism".[4]

The Fable of the Evil Impulse

Subsequently, the role of self-interest was explored at length in a Talmudic fable. This concludes that civilization is advanced through the operation of an "evil impulse" which is present in human nature. The fable is based on a story told in the *Babylonian Talmud*.[5]

The story involved is both dramatic and suspenseful. In it, the

[3] *Abot*, op. cit., Vol. I, Ch. 3. For background, see Y.I. Halevy, *Dorot HaRishonim* (Berlin: Herz, 1923), Part I, Vol. C., pp. 167, 171. Halevy writes: "Antigonus succeeded Simeon the Just as the 'Mufla of the Sanhedrin'." The "Mufla" was the Head Judge. Consult also, Z. Frankel, *Darkhei Ha-Mishnah*, pp. 28, 30. On the remuneration of members of the Sanhedrin, see Talmud Jerusalem, *Maaser Sheni*, Ch. V: 5, and Maimonides, *Shekalim*, 4: 7. The latter is quite explicit that the Sanhedrin, "received their salaries from the 'Office of Contributions'." This statement is based on Talmud, *Kethuboth*, 105a. Further to this background, it should be remarked that the fact that the Chief Judge of the Sanhedrin bore a Greek name (Antigonus) is some indication of the extent to which Hellenistic influence was present at this period.
[4] Joseph Schumpeter, *History of Economic Analysis* (New York: Oxford University Press, 1962), p. 66.
[5] Consult, *Babylonian Talmud*, *Yoma*, 69-b, *Sanhedrin* 64-a.

reader is transported back to a deeply moving event from circa 450 BCE as the Talmudic writers visualize how the returnees from the Babylonian captivity mourn their national disaster. The mood is sombre, but suddenly the narrative is transformed into a drama of universal import. Such a transformation is not surprising in the Talmud, since in the complex world of its text, the particular and the general, the logical and the theological, the national and the universal are interwoven in the manner of an oriental tapestry. In this instance, reflections which are national in character become universal in scope. Attention is directed to the significance of *Yetzer-Ha-rah*, the evil desire, tempter of idolatry, and, in this parable, to immoral action in general.[6]

A translation and paraphrase of the fable is given below. The literary form which we have chosen for its presentation is similar to that of Bernard Mandeville's celebrated *The Fable of the Bees*. (1705). This choice is not an arbitrary one, but is designed to emphasize the striking similarity of the views expressed in both fables. *The Fable of the Evil Impulse* reads, as follows:

> Alas, alas it is he! the idolatrous passion,
> Israel has been exiled, the sanctuary destroyed;
> The righteous were slain, no compassion . . .
> Yet still he is dancing amidst our void.
>
> Hast Thou planted in us the impulse to kiss
> That we may battle his tempting sword,
> To receive thereafter Thine eternal bliss?[7]
>
> The Heavens approved—a tablet fell down,
> "I agree"—it read—"you spoke the 'truth'".
> A three-day fast they ordered on their own,
> "Let's capture him and never let him loose".
>
> Suddenly he came forth from the Holy of Holies,
> A young lion aglow spitting with fire
> They wrestled with him to subdue their follies,
> He surrendered, roaring—"I lost a 'hair'"!!8
>
> Seeing that this is a time for heavenly Grace
> They prayed for mercy to hand them "Yetzer", the Base.

---

[6] For the etymological derivation of "Yetzer-Ha-rah", or "evil impulse", and its various meanings, see George Foot Moore, *Judaism* (Cambridge, Mass.: Harvard University Press, 1950) Vol. I., pp. 479–91.

[7] The thought here is that Israel would be rewarded for resisting the evil impulse.

[8] The "hair" is a metaphor for the biblical Easu (who was "all hairy"). It is also a metaphor for Easu's mentor-angel who was understood by the rabbis to be the "tempter of idolatry". Consult Samuel Edels (Maharsha), commentator *ad Talmud Yoma*, 69b.

As they triumphantly subdued the evil desire,
"Beware"!—the prophet thundered—
"If you kill him the world will expire"!

For three days the "Evil Yetzer" was imprisoned;
Temptations vanished, greed and pride ceased.
Hurrah! the battle over, the sex-impulse is won—

Alas . . . a fresh egg is needed, there is none.[9]
What shall we do?—they now intensely thought,
Shall we kill him? the world couldn't survive,
No one would build, nothing be sold or bought
Neither shall one marry, no children, no drive.[10]

At last it dawned—a truth profound
In scheme divine—a principle sound:
Vicious forces as passion, avarice and greed
Are vehicles of progress the world doth need.[11]
The tempter must live to tempt, so let no one dare
Deprive the Yetzer-Ha-Rah of his major glare.

Underlying the thought of this fable is the view that mankind has
been endowed with two diametrically opposed impulses.[12] These
two "souls"—the spiritual and the mundane, the virtuous and the
vicious—are present in each individual, and are designed to compete constantly with one another.[13] Both contend for a "reward"—
one in the realm of the material, the other in the domain of the
spiritual. In this second sphere, the "virtuous act" is seen as
constituting its own reward.[14] The competition between the two
"souls", or natures, is fierce. Yet, this does not lead the Talmudists

---

[9] On this observation, see Rashi, *Sanhedrin*, 64a. The normal temperature
necessary for procreation was reduced considerably both in male and female such
that even when the egg happened to ripen the chicken could not lay it.

[10] *Midrash Rabba*. (Jerusalem: Wahrman Books, 1965), Ch. 16. "Were it not for
the evil impulse, no man would build, procreate, or engage in business enterprise". See also, *Midrash Kohelet Rabba*, 4:4, and *Yalkut Shimoni*, Pardes ed. (1944),
Ch. 16:5, p. 9.

[11] *Midrash Tehilim*, Buber ed. (Jerusalem: Brothers Rom, 1967), Ch. 37, p. 272:
". . . God said . . . were it not for *Kinah* the world could not exist since no one
would marry or build a house . . ." The term *Kinah* connotes jealousy, envy,
passion, emulation. It is akin to "greed", "appetite", and "ambition". The
implication of the foregoing statement is that man was intended to behave in a
moderately "vicious" way that was socially expedient.

[12] *Babylonian Talmud, Brakhot* 61a. ". . . Two passions did God create, the good
and the bad . . ." The term "yetzer" or "inclination" is derived from the Biblical
"vayiitzar" (Genesis 2:7) with two vowels. From this it was inferred that God
"fashioned" man with "two natures".

[13] *Babylonian Talmud, Brakhot* 5a.

[14] Ibid., 61b. See also, *Babylonian Talmud, Abot* IV. II. "The reward of a good
deed is the deed itself". Although divine retribution was taken for granted by the
rabbis, they insisted that it should not serve as a primary motive for virtue.

to propose a dichotomy between the natural order and the moral order. Further, they do not draw a sharp line of demarkation between the holy and the profane.

Such a stance involves a number of problems, and one of these is highlighted by the fable. The complete attainment of moral perfection, it would appear, evokes unacceptable costs. Should pure "virtue" manage to render natural "vice" impotent, the result may be the destruction of an indispensible, equiliberating force in human society, and, perhaps, in the universe as a whole. As the Talmudic reflection indicates: "Vicious forces as passion, avarice, and greed are vehicles of progress the world doth need".

The inference from this latter is that although there are forces of a polarizing nature within any individual—benevolence and passion, righteousness and wickedness, ignorance and erudition—these forces are not necessarily mutually exclusive and may find some measure of common ground.[15] Hence, certain propensities which might be regarded as "evil", or morally debasing, are more correctly understood as "impulses" or natural instincts. In themselves, they are neither bad nor good. Rather, they are morally neutral. What matters is how the impulse or natural instinct is utilized by the individual person.

Mandeville's Fable and the Talmud

In the emergence of classical political economy in Europe during the late eighteenth century considerable emphasis was placed on the idea that the exercise of enlightened self-interest was efficacious. Essentially selfish behaviour, it was contended, could be conducive to the benefit of society as a whole. This idea was central to the new, liberal economics of Adam Smith and it was anticipated by an earlier philosopher, Bernard de Mandeville (1670–1733).

Mandeville's "poem" *The Grumbling Hive* (1705), which was renamed *The Fable of the Bees*, shocked many of his contemporaries.[16]

---

[15] There is a variety of passages bearing on this theme. For example, *Talmud, Haggiga* 15a states: "Whatever God created, He also created its counterpart". *Babylonian Talmud, Brakhot* 61b declares: ". . . The world has been created only for the wholly wicked or wholly righteous (to be enjoyed)." According to *Zohar, Tazria* 47: "Were it not for the existence of ignorance there would be no erudition"; "Without wickedness there would be no conception of righteousness"; and, "brilliance could hardly be conceived without darkness." The *Zohar* or "Splendour" is a kabalistic work which deals with mystical psychology. It is based upon discussions of a group of second century rabbis.

[16] Bernard de Mandeville, *The Fable of the Bees, or Private Vices, Public Benefits*, with a commentary by F.B. Kaye (Oxford: Clarendon Press, 1924), 2 vols.

However, its leading thesis would not have shocked the Talmudic scholars of earlier centuries. Mandeville found that vice and virtue, although distinctly opposed categories, tend to interact and can reinforce each other. The Talmudists, as we have seen, had arrived at this insight long before. Unlike Mandeville, the rabbis contended that individual persons have the capacity to act from motives that are "pure". They did not reject the possibility of altruism. On the other hand, there is fundamental agreement between Mandeville and the rabbis when it comes to the psychologizing of economic phenomena.

According to Mandeville, human societies exhibit a striking paradox. Namely:

> Parties directly opposite
> Assist each other as 'twere for spite.[17]

The apparently discordant passions harmonize to the end that "private vices" are turned into "public benefits". To substantiate this assertion, Mandeville leads his readers through the tortuous dealings of merchants and lawyers, priests and judges, moralists and politicians, who, he finds, are all vicious. Yet, their wickedness forms the stuff out of which a benevolent social fabric is fashioned. Mandeville writes:

> Millions endeavouring to supply
> Each others' Lust and Vanity . . .[18]
> Thus every Part was full of Vice,
> Yet the whole Mass a Paradise.[19]

All material civilization, then, is the product of vices gratified. It is not the fruit of virtue. This suggests that it is the consequences of men's actions which are important rather than the motives involved. Even base motives result in actions which are usually beneficial and agreeable to society.

Mandeville went on to amplify his views in a series of prose essays. During the course of these he affirms, "how necessary our appetites and passions are for the welfare of Trade and Handicraft", and he observes that, "Avarice and Prodigality are equally necessary to society".[20] He reasons that in the final analysis, "a Passion in our Nature . . . may be Good or Bad according to the

---

[17] Mandeville, op. cit. Also *The Grumbling Hive* (Oxford: Clarendon Press, 1924), p. 25.
[18] *Fable*, op. cit., i, 18.
[19] Ibid., i, 24.
[20] Ibid., *Remarks*, p. 250.

Actions perform'd."[21] Such observations are highly supportive of the view that economic progress will be enhanced if free play is given to the pursuit of selfish ends. The vice of selfishness will spur each individual on to maximize his or her gains, thereby contributing to the growth of the wealth of a society.

It is evident then that both Mandeville and the Talmudists regard the natural impulse as a constructive force which makes for gains in social utility. In fact, the Talmudists are prepared to go to the same lengths as does Mandeville in emphasizing the social element. This occurs at the point where they differentiate between the "good" and the "very good" natural impulse.

In the *Midrash*, the very good natural impulse is associated quite explicitly with the "evil passion". The rabbis ask: "But can the evil passion be *very good*?" The answer is in the affirmative. The reasons given for this answer are that if it were not for the evil passion, no one would marry, neither build nor engage in business, and, "the world could not exist."[22] Here, the *Aggadic* rendition places the "evil", i.e., natural, instinct on a higher plane than the good impulse. This somewhat surprising elevation appears to be due to the utilitarian (in the broad sense) function of the evil instinct.

Mandeville adopts the same stance. He writes:

> Envy itself and Vanity
> Were Ministers of Industry[23]

> As Price and Luxury decrease
> So by degrees they leave the Seas . . .
> All Arts and Crafts neglected lie;
> Content, the Bane of Industry
> Makes 'em admire their homely Store
> And neither Seek nor Covet more.[24]

> Fraud, Luxury and pride must live
> While we the Benefits receive.[25]

For the Talmudic writers, as for Mandeville, mankind's propensity to marry, truck and build is a product of the natural impulse. Hence forces such as passion, ambition and greed, which are necessarily associated with that impulse, are indispensable instruments maintaining the world in operational balance. Such forces are utilitarian vehicles for the advance of civilization. Virtue

---

[21] Ibid., p. 74.
[22] *Kohelet Rabba*, 4:4.
[23] *Fable*, op. cit., p. 25.
[24] Ibid., i, 34–5.
[25] Ibid., i, 36–7.

without vice is counter-productive. Within the diversity of man's
motives there is uniformity of design. An operational balance serves
to harmonize individual strivings with the interests of society.

Other-Directed Action

There are many historians of economic thought who have contended that there is a direct link between the writings of Mandeville
and the economic liberalism of Adam Smith. For example, Charles
Gide wrote:

> Smith criticised Mandeville in his *Theory of Moral Sentiments*. But
> despite his criticism, Mandeville's idea bore fruit in Smith's mind.
> Smith in his turn was to reiterate the belief that it was personal
> interest (in his opinion, not vice, but an inferior virtue) that unwit-
> tingly led society to the path of well-being and prosperity. A nation's
> wealth for Smith, as well as for Mandeville, is the result, if not of a
> vice, at least of a natural instinct . . . which is bestowed upon us by
> Providence for the realization of ends that lie beyond our farthest
> ken.[26]

Given that link, it is apparent that the talmudic scholars must be
accounted notable anticipators of a set of ideas which is central to
Smith's economic philosophy, and this, despite the fact that there is
no evidence that Smith had any direct acquaintance with the
Talmudic tradition. However, the points of contact between ideas
in that tradition and Smith's philosophy go beyond those that have
been considered thus far. The contacts are not confined to insights
which the writings of Mandeville illustrate.

Further affiliations between the ideas of Smith and those of the
rabbis derive from the latter's other-directed theory of human
action. With this theory, it is not a question of mankind's instincts,
as above. Rather, it is the issue of the place of conscious motives
and their relationship to humanity's creative potential. The theory
also evokes debate concerning the presence of a guiding spirit in
human affairs, which spirit makes for economic interdependence.

Underlying the Talmudic approach to creative action is the
belief that the presence of such action in human affairs is providential. It is Providence which is the force behind mankind's drive to
create. Hence, in a *Midrashic* statement, Providence is portrayed as
a calling upon Israel to plant and build. The statement reads, in
part:

---

[26] Charles Gide and Charles Rist, *A History of Economic Doctrines* (London:
Heath, 1913), p. 72.

"Even though thou mayest find the land prosperous, thou must not recoil saying: 'I shall relax and refrain from planting' . . . Just as thou hast found plantations which others have established before you, thou must do the same for posterity . . . Do not say . . . why should I labour for others . . .?"[27]

In this passage, providence is depicted as prodding mankind to rationalize its economic activities. It is as if Providence is saying: "How much less fortunate would you be without your ancestors' sweat and toil. You in turn must do the same for the coming generation". The import is that any one generation "builds" or "plants" partly on the basis of its awareness of an inevitable interdependence in economic life. Providence ensures that the self-interested, creative action of a generation can be consciously "other-directed".

The *Midrashic* statement does not end at this point, however. It continues on to a psychological explanation of creative endeavour. The rabbis add:

"Were it not for the concealment of death from man's heart, he would neither build nor plant, claiming, 'tomorrow I die, why should I toil for others?' Therefore has Providence concealed from man the day of his death so that he would continue to build . . . Now if he be worthy he himself will be the beneficiary; if not, he will serve as a benefactor *L'Ahayrim*, to others."[28]

In this second part of the statement, the *Midrash* treats the individual person as a selfish creature. Were it not for expectations of personal comfort and pleasure, real or imaginary, the individual would refrain from productive activity. If he or she does engage in creative endeavour, it is because of economic self-interest.

This point established, the *Midrash* proceeds to unveil an aspect of the other-directed character of human action which differs from the previous inter-generational consideration. As is stated, if a person merits ("if he be worthy") that person will enjoy personally the fruit of his or her labour. On the other hand, if a person does not merit, then *L'Ahayrim*, he or she becomes society's benefactor. A person may be motivated simply by total self-interest, but the results of that individual's endeavours may serve the interests of others. His or her action is unconsciously "other-directed".[29]

---

[27] *Midrash-Tanhuma, K'doshim* 8, Horeb, ed. (Leipzig, 1927). *Tanhuma* is the oldest *Aggadic Midrash*. According to S. Buber, publisher of the oldest text (Vilna, 1885), it antedates the *Babylonian Talmud*.

[28] Ibid.

[29] The Midrash also illustrates this point by way of the following incident: The Roman Emperor Hadrian (2nd cent.) while touring Palestine, noticed a very old

Taken together, the two parts of the foregoing *Midrashic* statement embrace both action based on sympathetic feelings towards
society and action based on unalloyed self-interest. The role of
Providence is relevant in both cases. In the first, man's conscience
is prodded by Divine Providence to be concerned with the feelings
and reactions of other persons. Some of these others have built and
planted before, so how can one do otherwise? The recommendation
is: "Do not say, why should I work for others?" The emphasis here
is on man's congenial feeling for the maintenance of harmony in
human affairs. By contrast, the second part of the statement turns
on the notion that man is basically selfish. Yet despite this, Providence has arranged for a proportion of mankind's self-interested
activity to result in public benefit. Those who are not themselves
"worthy" can be society's providential benefactors.

Affiliations with Smith

The other-directed theory of human action as developed by the
Talmudists has its counterparts in the thought of Adam Smith. The
aspect of that theory which encompasses action based on sympathetic feelings toward society is represented most clearly in
Smith's *Theory of Moral Sentiments* (1759). In that book, Smith
contends that ethical systems develop by a natural process out of
individual personal relationships. The individual decides that certain actions are proper or improper by observing the reactions of
others to his or her behaviour. A social consensus then develops
that approves those patterns of behaviour which benefit both the
individual and society. Here, Smith's emphasis is on the significance of "fellow feeling" as a social force. This same emphasis is
evident when the *Aggadic Midrash* directs attention to the action
appropriate to reflection on what the individual has gained in
economic terms from the efforts of others.

A second aspect of the talmudic theory was based on the assumption of the predominance of activity which is entirely self-
interested. This line of analysis has more in common with that of

---

Jew planting fig trees. "You old man"—he asked—"why are you working in vain?
Do you believe that you will eat the fruit of your labor?" The old man replied: "If I
will be deserving, I will eat the fruits, and if not, let my children eat them."

Elsewhere in the *Talmud*, one rabbi recommends consciously other directed
action in aid of maximizing economic self-interest. This occurs in a *Aggadic*
rendition of a Biblical exhortation to be charitable to the indigent (*Deuteronomy*,
14:22): "Said, R. Johanan, 'Aser B'shvil Sh'tisasher' (Thou shalt surely tithe in
order that thou become rich)." *Babylonian Talmud*, Taanit, 9a. This recommendation appears also in *Shabbat*, 119a.

Adam Smith in his *Wealth of Nations* (1776). In this book Smith depicts the individual as continually exerting himself to discover the most personally advantageous employment for both himself and his capital. Further, as in the *Haggadic* understanding, Smith perceives that this self-dedicated individual may often be the un-witting benefactor of society at large. Such an individual, Smith writes, "neither intends to promote the public interest, nor knows how much he is promoting it . . . he is . . . led by an invisible hand to promote an end which was no part of his intention . . . By pursuing his own interest he frequently promotes that of society."[30]

The rabbis, it is clear, would find nothing strange in Smith's doctrine of an "invisible hand". That hand, in their understanding, is the hand of Divine Providence which has deliberately fashioned human nature to produce the sort of unintended consequences which impressed Smith. Their concept of the order within Creation may not be co-extensive with Smith's "natural order", but both concepts relate the economic interests of the individual to those of society, partly by reference to unintended consequences.

In the earlier sections of this chapter we demonstrated the strong affinity between the thought of the Talmudic fable of the evil impulse and the Mandeville-Smith position on self-interest and national wealth. The latter sections show the striking resemblance of the *Haggadic* treatment of economic action to that which under-lies Smith's advocacy of economic liberalism. The chapters which follow take the investigation of rabbinic insights into more particu-lar areas of economic enquiry.

---

[30] Adam Smith, *An Inquiry into the Nature and Causes of the Wealth of Nations*, edited by Edwin Cannan, (London, 1904), p. 421.

CHAPTER FOUR

SCARCITY, SUPPLY AND FLUCTUATIONS

For most modern economists, *the* economic problem is the problem of scarcity. In this respect, those economists follow the understanding of Lord Robbins in his influential, *An Essay on the Nature and Significance of Economic Science* (1932). This chapter shows that the talmudists were no strangers to the idea that scarcity is a fundamental feature of the human condition. The idea was prominent in the earliest books of Jewish literature, and it remained a basic point of reference for the rabbis. Further, it is shown that the talmudic scholars probed the problem of scarcity by way of analysis of failures in the supply of commodities. These probings included an approach to the beginnings of a theory of economic fluctuations, plus some strong intimations of a quantity theory of money.

The Problem of Scarcity

From almost its outset, the biblical book of *Genesis* (circa, 900 B.C.E.) is concerned to emphasize the problem of scarcity. In that book, as Adam and Eve depart the Garden of Eden, the Lord informs Adam:

> Cursed is the ground for thy sake; in sorrow shalt thou eat of it all the days of thy life. Thorns and thistles shall it bring forth to thee; and thou shalt eat the herb of the field. In the sweat of the face shalt thou eat bread. (*Genesis*, 3:17–19).

For the writer, or writers, of *Genesis*, mankind has chosen to tend to its consumption needs in an independent fashion, rather than leave the matter to the benevolence of its Creator. Hence, mankind is obliged to foresake the Garden as part of the logic of this choice. Mankind has embraced the problem of wresting its subsistence from the earth at the cost of personal toil and trouble ("the sweat of thy face"). It has committed itself to coming to grips with a Nature that might prove niggardly and with environments that could be inhospitable. This circumstance, it is emphasized, was not the Creator's intention. Nevertheless, the Creator is prepared to honour mankind's choice to be responsible itself for the production of the goods and services which will sustain it.[1]

---

[1] For more extensive analysis of *Genesis* on these issues see, B. Gordon, *The Economic Problem in Biblical and Patristic Thought* (Leiden: E.J. Brill, 1989), pp. 1–5.

This vision of the human condition continues in the *Talmud*. For example, Simeon B. Elezar (c. 165–200 C.E.) asks:

> Hast thou ever seen a wild animal or a bird practising a craft?—Yet they have their sustenance without care and were they created for naught else but to serve me? But I was created to serve my Maker. How much more then ought not I to have my sustenance without care?[2]

Rabbi Simeon answers his own question: "But I have wrought evil, and so forfeited my right to sustenance without care". The observations from other scholars which accompany this answer recommend the engagement in a "cleanly craft" to take care of the individual's need of subsistence. At the same time, these caution that economic success is a matter of the craftsman's degree of moral worth rather than the technical skill which he comes to command. It is command of the Law which is most beneficial since, "a man enjoys the reward thereof in this world and its whole worth remains for the world to come." (*Kiddushin*, 4:14). The best way of dealing with the problem of scarcity on an individual basis is to take care to attain knowledge of the Law, and to be careful in its observance.

Failure of Supply

Whereas the biblical treatment of scarcity is couched mainly in terms that are either quite general or person-specific, the *Talmud* engages in social analysis of the phenomenon. It distinguishes between different types of scarcity which can afflict a particular community. One of these is *Batzoret* which arises from structural causes. The other, *Kafna*, is a much more serious eventuality. This involves a negative shift in the total supply of essential commodities.[3]

The problem of *Batzoret* is mainly a problem of distribution which impacts on market price. It assumes no change in aggregate supply. Yields are normal in this instance, but there may be some disturbance in the distribution system which prevents it from working in the accustomed manner. The local transportation system, for example, may not be able to function as usual.[4] Here, there will be

---

[2] *Kiddushin*, 4:14.

[3] *Babylonian Talmud, Tractate Taanit*, p. 19b. The discussion of *Batzoret* and *Kafna* which follows is based on the original analysis first published in R.A. Ohrenstein, "Economic Thought in Talmudic Literature in the Light of Modern Economics," *American Journal of Economics and Sociology*, 27 (1968), pp. 185–96.

[4] C.f., *Tossafoth, Tractate Taanit*, p. 19a. The *Tossafoth* is a composite commentary by the disciples of Rashi (d. 1105) which supplements that of their master.

localized shortages which need to be made good by importation from other regions. Also, the price level will rise, if only because of additional transport costs.

Kafna, by contrast, involves a failure in aggregate supply engendered by climatic factors or by a major disruption to transport.[5] In this instance, the talmudists are contemplating a condition which would be represented in a modern Economics textbook by a substantial, inward shift of the normal supply curve. A certain quantity of product will be forthcoming on the market only at a price per unit that is well in excess of what pertains in most seasons.

The rabbis recognize that *Kafna* is qualitatively distinct from *Batzoret*. *Kafna* may require the implementation of emergency measures to sustain the populace. Fluctuations in supply can be so serious as to demand intervention to prevent market outcomes from spelling social disaster.

Prosperity and Depression

Further exploration of the distinction between *Batzoret* and *Kafna* led the talmudists into more extensive examination of the functional relationships between economic variables. Their focus, in this regard, was on the behaviour of a regional economy as a whole. Hence, they came to realize that the issues which concerned them could not be resolved without reference to the monetary circumstances of the region in question.

The opening move in the widening debate was made by Rabbi Hanina (third century, C.E.). In distinguishing between *Batzoret* and *Kafna*, he observed:

"If a *Se'ah* of grain costs one *Sela'* and is obtainable—it is *Batzoret*; but if four *Se'ahs* cost a *Sela'* but are not easily obtainable then it is *Kafna*".[6]

A *Se'ah* was a measurement of quantity which approximated thirteen litres, and a *Sela'* was a monetary unit with an exchange value of four silver *dinarii*. The Rabbi is claiming then, that when a certain quantity commands a particular price and is freely available for purchase this indicates a shortfall of supply due to distributional problems that are not of major consequence. On the other

---

[5] In terms of ancient economic thought, the transport issue loomed large, and locational issues could often be paramount. The rabbis, for example, were looking to situations in which the flow of products was a matter of conveyance by means of rivers or canals. Inadequate water levels could be major variables conditioning market circumstances.

[6] *Babylonian Talmud, Tractate Taanit*, p. 19b.

hand, when that same quantity commands a much lower price but is less readily purchased by the consumer then there is a major scarcity problem which justifies emergency measures.

Hanina's statement might be dismissed as illogical, since he envisages that a commodity will be unobtainable despite a fall of 300 per cent in its price, whereas it is available despite a price increase of 300 per cent.[7] Yet, Rabbi Johanan (mid-third century, C.E.) finds the statement logical. Johanan explains:

"This applies only in a situation when money is cheap and commodities are dear, but when money is dear and commodities are cheap, a state of emergency is declared at once".[8]

Here, Johanan is pointing to the fact that because one measure of grain costs as much as a *Sela'*, or because price may fall by as much as 300 per cent, these do not of themselves indicate the true nature of the scarcity problem at these times. There can be other economic variables at work such that a shortfall of supply is more apparent than real. The true reason for the variations in price level could be bound up with monetary factors, i.e., with inflation or deflation.

Johanan seems to have appreciated that economies can be subject to alternating periods of prosperity and depression. He states that there are phases when money is cheap and commodities are dear, as well as phases when money is dear and commodities cheap. In times of prosperity, he reasons, business is brisk, and, as a tenth century commentator, Rabbi Hananel, adds, personal income is on the rise. Money is in greater abundance, and it tends to become cheaper in terms of other commodities. The money prices of those other commodities rise.

These insights permit Johanan to understand Hanina's position that when a *Se'ah* of grain costs one *Sela'*, it was not a time for emergency measures. The current price reflected the bouyancy of business and increased personal incomes. *Batzoret* for Johanan signifies price inflation, and since that is a characteristic of a period of prosperity, the state of the market price for grain is not an object of grave concern for the authorities. In times of prosperity, prices may rise as much as threefold, but so might personal incomes.

On the other hand, Johanan appreciates Hanina's depiction of *Kafna*. This appreciation is based partly on personal experience. Johanan reminiscenses:

> I distinctly recall when one could have obtained *four* measures for one *Sela'*, yet people were starving in Tiberias for want of a penny (an *isar*).

---

[7] Here, we express the percentage change as a calculation from its base.
[8] Ibid., p. 19b.

In this situation, money was dear. Commodities appeared to be in plentiful supply, but few could aspire to buy them. Here was a set of circumstances which could justify the proclamation of a state of emergency. Prices had fallen threefold, but it would seem that personal incomes had been depressed to an even greater degree.

The Quantity Theory of Money

The foregoing analyses of prosperity and depression by R. Johanan and his successors clearly involve engagement in monetary issues at the macro-economic level. Further, that engagement, with its recognition of the existence of a quantitative relationship between money supply and prices (and, between prices and incomes), suggests that the rabbis had come to appreciate the fundamentals of what was to emerge later as the quantity theory of money.[9]

R. Johanan, as we have seen, finds a definite, quantitative relationship between money and prices. Then, as elucidated by R. Hananel, the relationship between money and prices turns on a change in community incomes, since an increase in those incomes engenders a greater volume of currency in circulation. Such reasoning embodies the theoretical ingredients of a quantity approach. Even further, it might be claimed that Johanan subscribed to a rather more sophisticated version of the quantity theory than that which was adopted in the orthodox political economy of the early nineteenth century. For James Mill, David Ricardo and others, changes in the money supply lead to *proportional* changes in the general price level. However, in his reflections on the depression in Tiberias (noted above), Johanan seems to envisage a *disproportionate* relationship between the quantity of money in circulation and

---

[9] In the literature of Economics there are several variants of the quantity theory. However, each affirms that *ceteris paribus* an increase in the quantity of money will tend to decrease the purchasing power of the unit of currency. C.f., J.A. Schumpeter, *History of Economic Analysis* (New York: Oxford University Press, 1954), p. 703. The first clear statement of that theory was made by the Spanish theologian Martin Azplicueta Navarrus in 1556 C.E. Navarrus wrote: ". . . other things being equal, in countries where there is a great scarcity of money all other saleable goods, and even the hands and labour of men, are given for less money than where it is abundant. Thus, we see by experience that in France, where money is scarcer than in Spain, bread, wine, cloth and labour are worth much less. And even in Spain, in times when money was scarcer, saleable goods and labour were given for very much less than after the discovery of the Indies, which flooded the country with gold and silver. The reason for this is that money is worth more where and when it is scarce than where and when it is abundant." Consult, M. Grice-Hutchinson, *The School of Salamanca* (Oxford: Clarendon Press, 1952), p. 52, and p. 95.

market prices, where the variation in that quantity is a function of the general business conditions prevailing. Perhaps, Johanan's conception is in consonance with the post-classical rather than the classical understanding of the matter.

Cycles, Stars and Harvests

From the above, it is clear that Rabbi Johanan recognized that business conditions in regional economies can fluctuate. Such a recognition prompts the question as to whether or not Johanan, or some of his talmudic successors, offered any explanation for such fluctuations. It emerges that it is highly likely that the rabbis came to understand business fluctuations in terms of what later was called the "harvest-theory" of cycles in economic activity. This type of theory attributes cycles to the effect on a region's total income of alternating periods of good and bad harvests.

As Joseph Schumpeter has observed, "the most exogenous of all factors that influence economic life is variation of harvest in so far as due to weather, a factor pressed into service for the purpose of explaining business fluctuations by W.S. Jevons, H.S. Jevons (his son), and H.L. Moore."[10] The publications to which Schumpeter is referring are: W.S. Jevons, *Investigations in Currency and Finance* (1884); H.S. Jevons, *The Sun's Heat and Trade Activity* (1910); and, H.L. Moore, *Economic Cycles: Their Law and Cause* (1914). This line of analysis was anticipated earlier in the nineteenth century by Thomas Tooke and by the French economist Briaune, and Schumpeter notes also that as early as 1662 Sir William Petty used the term "cycle" with reference to the sequence of good and bad harvests.[11]

In essence, the harvest theory links prosperity and depression in the economy to the fortunes of the agricultural sector. Those fortunes are linked in turn to the state of the weather. Hence the physical determinants of cycles in weather patterns have a causal relationship with the condition of the economy as a whole. W.S. Jevons, for example, focussed on sun-spot activity.

Did Rabbi Johanan subscribe to this set of linkages? Certainly, his analysis of *Batzoret* and *Kafna* demonstrates that he associates fluctuations in the condition of the economy as a whole with those of agricultural production and supply. Further, it is the case that

---

[10] J.A. Schumpeter, *History of Economic Analysis* (New York: Oxford University Press, 1954), p. 1133. See also, pp. 876–77, on H.L. Moore.
[11] Ibid., pp. 742–45.

elsewhere in his expositions Johanan encourages physical scientific enquiry with respect to solar periods. A leading statement is, as follows:

"Said R. Johanan: whence do we know that it is incumbent upon every person to calculate the cycles of the seasons and constellations? For it is stated (Dt. 4:5–8): '. . . keep them, obey them, for this is your wisdom and intelligence in the sight of the nations.'— What kind of wisdom is in the *sight* of the nations? It is the science of the solar periods and constellations."[12]

Here, Johanan is recommending the collection of scientific data on solar phenomena, a recommendation which is emphasized by his stress on the noun "sight". However, why collect the data? His reference to "the cycles of the seasons and constellations" suggests that the wisdom gained is of importance for prediction of the weather. Nevertheless, this point is not absolutely clear from the text.

Clarification of Johanan's position is undertaken by the authoritative talmudic interpreter, Rashi (eleventh century). He remarks on his predecessor's rendition of the biblical phrase, "in the sight of the nations," in the following passage:

"It directs our attention to the kind of wisdom which is observable and (scientifically) verifiable, namely, the calculation of the course of the sun and constellations, *which tell us whether a given year will be rainy or subject to drought* [emphasis added], since all the periods are determined by the sun and constellations."[13]

Rashi is in no doubt as to why the information should be collected. The information bears directly on the weather that can be expected. Rashi's clarification is also of interest in terms of later business cycle theory because of its specification of the sun, rather than the moon, as the prime object of systematic investigation. This specification, it can be added, is entirely in conformity with the tradition to which he was heir. Professor Power writes:

"The Hebrew year was not lunar but lunisolar. This was necessitated by the harvest offerings at the annual feasts since harvest time is regulated by the sun. Another month, therefore, Adar II (Ve-Adar), was intercalated before Nisan [March–April] if further time was needed for the ripening of the barley first-fruits to be offered during the feast of the Pasch [April]."[14]

---

[12] *Tractate Sabbat*, 75a. The translation of this passage is by the authors.
[13] Ibid. Translation by the authors.
[14] E. Power, "Measures, Weights, Money and Time", in B. Orchard et al. (eds.), *A Catholic Commentary on Holy Scripture* (London: Nelson, 1953), p. 112.

Additional emphasis on the role of the sun in terms of weather conditions is provided by a later talmudic commentator who is known as the "Maharsha" (1555–1631). This commentator is also impressed by the need for systematic investigation of the physical phenomena involved. In his *Legal Novellae*, Maharsha affirms that it is the sun which determines whether or not seasonal conditions will be wet or dry. Further, the acquisition of wisdom in this field, "is both theoretical and empirical, subject to exact calculations, just as the astronomers who employ scientific instruments to observe the movements of the sun and constellations." (*Hiddushai Halakhot, Sabb.*, p. 42).

When the insights of Rabbi Johanan are put together with the comments of Rashi and the Maharsha, there is a strong case for the contention that the talmudic tradition fostered a harvest-cycle theory of business fluctuations. Even more specifically, it would seem that the tradition directed attention to scientific investigation of solar phenomena as providing the basis for knowledge of the incidence of prosperity and depression.[15] In this regard, the tradition may be said to have anticipated an aspect of later economic thought which is associated, in particular, with the research of W.S. Jevons.[16]

Talmudic sources demonstrate that the intercalation of the years was a practice of the Sanhedrin in the Hasmonean and Mishnaic periods. On the various reasons offered for intercalation, see, *Tractate Sanhedrin*, 11a ff., and *Tosef, Sanh.* 2:12.

[15] C.f., *Genesis Rabbah* (s. 10): ". . . there is no herb which has not a planet in heaven that strikes it and says: 'grow'."

[16] It can be added that it might be some recognition of the existence of agricultural cycles which underlies the biblical institutions of *Shmitah* and *Yovel*. The first of these assumes a duration of seven years, and the second, fifty years. This second duration is approximately that ascribed to "long waves" by the Russian economist N.D. Kondratieff.

PART THREE

MICRO-ECONOMIC ISSUES

CHAPTER FIVE

OPPORTUNITY COST AND MARKET BEHAVIOUR

Parallels between talmudic analysis and later developments in Economics are not confined to insights associated with macro-economic issues. In this chapter (as in Chapter Six) we show that the rabbis anticipated aspects of micro-economics, as well. It is demonstrated that the talmudic concept of *S'khar B'teilo*, or "lost time", looks forward to the neo-classical innovation which came to be known as "opportunity cost". Also relevant here is a controversy, reported in the Jerusalem Talmud, concerning loss of business opportunity.

Further, in their explorations of the operation of free-market mechanisms, the Jewish scholars distinguished many of the phenomena that have come to be recognized as significant for an understanding of the economics of markets. For example, they understood the difference between price and non-price competition, the role of product differentiation, and the manner in which expectations can influence price. They also considered the role of demand in price formation.

Opportunity Cost

The classical economics of Adam Smith and his successors was marked by an adherence to the doctrine of "real" cost. In economic terms, the cost of any item consists of the toil and trouble which it takes to produce or acquire the item in question. Further, if markets are genuinely free, the prices at which goods sell will tend to reflect their real costs.

During the neo-classical era, the Cambridge economist Alfred Marshall continued to hold to the doctrine of his British predecessors. However, on the Continent, the Austrian Friedrich von Wieser proposed an alternate approach. The actual phrase, "opportunity cost", was first employed by an American economist, H.J. Davenport (1861–1931).[1] Nevertheless, von Wieser was the first to explain what was involved, in his book *Natural Value* (1889). A subsequent explanation by von Wieser reads:

---

[1] H.J. Davenport, *The Economics of Enterprise* (New York, 1913).

Whenever the business man speaks of incurring costs, he has in mind the quantity of productive means required to achieve a certain end; but the associated idea of a sacrifice which his effort demands is also aroused. In what does this sacrifice consist? . . . The sacrifice consists in the exclusion or limitation of possibilities by which the other products might have been turned out, had the material not been devoted to one particular product. Our definition in an earlier connection made clear that cost-productive-means are productive agents which are widely scattered and have manifold uses. As such, they promise a profitable yield in many directions. But the realization of one of these necessarily involves a loss of all others. It is this sacrifice that is predicated in the concept of costs; the costs of production or the quantities of cost-productive-means required for a given product and thus withheld from other uses . . .[2]

To put this pioneer explanation in more succinct terms, it can be said that, the cost of devoting resources to one particular line of production is measured by the benefits foregone by not devoting them to an alternate line of use. This is a radically different understanding of "cost" from that which the British tradition affirmed. It is an understanding, however, which was shared by the talmudists.

The Concept of S'khar B'teilo (Lost Time)

The law of *S'khar B'teilo* deals with the problem of remuneration of a teacher of sacred lore (Torah), and the manner in which that problem is handled is in marked contrast with the approach suggested by the thought of Adam Smith. He was prepared to classify such teachers, together with university lecturers like himself, as "unproductive". Many of the most admirable persons in society, according to Smith, must be regarded as unproductive from an economist's perspective.[3] The rabbis, however, were not prepared to divorce their activities in such an uncompromising manner from the economic life of a community. They coped with the question of remuneration in Austrian, rather than Smithian, terms.

In ancient Jewish tradition it was held that a religious teacher, or judge, should not be compensated for his work. One ought not professionalize the Torah. A person must not derive material benefit from involvement with understanding and explication of sacred love. Yet, there came a point at which the ancient tradition could not be sustained. Elaborations of the implications of the Torah bourgeoned, hence specialization became an imperative.

---

[2] F. von Wieser, *Social Economics* (1914; trans., A. Ford Hindrichs, New York, 1927), p. 128.

[3] A. Smith, *The Wealth of Nations* (1776; New York, 1937), p. 315.

Remuneration for the specialist was acknowledged to be legitimate.[4]

For an economist, the most striking element in this transition to professional payment is the acknowledgement of the factor of a teacher's "lost time". This acknowledgement is explained in terms of *Agar B'teilo*, which is the Aramaic equivalent of the Hebrew *S'khar B'teilo*. Here, the teaching professional is recognized to be foregoing opportunities for personal economic gain because of his devotion of time to communication of Torah. The foregone opportunities warrant recompense.

The basis of the concept of *S'khar B'teilo* can be traced to the *Jerusalem Talmud* (1–5 C.E.) where, as a point of departure from the established rule, it is stated:

"V'khein khamiya nosvin agreyhon, amar Rav (Yodin B'rab) Yishmael, S'khar B'teilon heim notling." (We can readily observe that instructors actually do receive compensation, to which Rabbi Yishmael [second century] remarked: "They are being compensated for their loss of time.").[5]

The clear implication of this statement is that time is scarce and human resources limited. If knowledge were unlimited there would be no opportunity cost.

In the *Babylonian Talmud*, a medieval commentator, Rabbi Nissim Gerondi (1320–1380) quotes the *Jerusalem Talmud* as the source of the law in question.[6] Further, *Tractate Kiddushin* comments that *S'khar B'teilo* can be understood as, "a compensation for suspended work."[7] However, it is Rabbi Obadio Bartinoro (fifteenth century) who is quite explicit on the subject of "loss of time." Bartinoro puts the issue in unambiguous terms:

"Khamo mafsid m'bitul m'lakhto." (How much would a teacher have lost—or, could have earned—had he engaged in other gainful employment?)

Rabbi Bartinoro assigns a monetary or market value to the teacher's sacrifice, i.e., to the amount which the teacher could have earned in other alternative uses of his time. A century later, Rabbi Joseph Karo further crystallized the principle of "loss of time" by explicitly referring to *Masso-Mattan*, or "business dealings". This step represents a realization that there is nothing special, from the economic viewpoint, about the use of time by the learned. That use

---

[4] See, Arukh Ha-Shulhan, *Hilkot Talmud Torah*, p. 246.

[5] *T. Jerusalem*, Ned., Ch. 4, 14b.

[6] *Babylonian Talmud, Tractate Nedarim*, p. 37a.

[7] *Babylonian Talmud, Tractate Kiddushin*, p. 16b. See also, Rashi's explanation (eleventh century), ibid., p. 16b. Also consult, *Tractate Baba Mezia*, p. 68b.

is subject to the general consideration that time is a scarce resource, and any one use of time involves cost for the rabbi involved. A person adept in Torah may also be capable of commercial expertise, and this latter potentiality has a bearing on what he is worth as a teacher. As remarked above, Adam Smith tried to keep apart the worlds of scholarship and commerce. The logic of an opportunity-cost approach to remuneration, as Rabbi Karo realized, does not permit such a divorce.

Evaluation of Lost Time

The *Talmud* does not rest at the point of distinguishing the presence of foregone opportunities in questions of remuneration. It goes on to seek to establish concrete, monetary equivalents for the sacrifices which the opportunity cost approach emphasizes as relevant. This particular analytical endeavour by the talmudists is located in *Baba Mezia*, 76b–77a. Here the problem is that of wage-earners who have been engaged by an entrepreneur to transport a cargo. The entrepreneur cancels the agreement. Can the disengaged employees claim some compensation in this instance?

The talmudic scholars address this problem in economic justice by examination of the various conditions surrounding the initial contract of employment. They then establish the responsibilities of each party for the breach of contract. Eventually, they arrive at a consensus concerning the monetary award due the workers involved. This consensus incorporates equivalents for foregone opportunities. The decision includes a striking departure in terms of earlier economic thought in that it extends to the placing of a price on leisure.

In their pioneering judgement, the rabbis contemplate partial compensation for some of the workers involved. The equivalent of this compensation is deemed to be a *Poel Botel*. The scholars explain it in terms of: "How much less than the usual wages would a worker be prepared to accept in order to enjoy a leisurely rest?" Leisure, then, has a price on account of its foregone opportunity.

On and beyond this foregoing query, the analysis includes the rather more conventional question of the incidence of compensation in full. This question is understood to apply where the workers had already brought tools of trade plus material to the workplace. It is also construed to apply to a different group of workers, the *Mahoza* teamsters. The enforced idleness of the teamsters is treated as a total loss when their prospective job does not eventuate. Idleness to them is a "trial". In other words, it is seen as psychologically debilitating to be denied the opportunity to work when one is willing.

This latter observation, it should be remarked, is in direct accord with the biblical view that the act of working, in itself, has some positive utility for the worker. According to the *Book of Genesis*, mankind is made in the image of the God who works. Even in the Garden of Eden, before mankind sins, and becomes subject to the problem of scarcity, man and woman are workers. Mankind is intended by the Creator to gain pleasure from work itself.[8] It is understandable then, that the rabbis find enforced idleness warrants compensation for the foregone utilities involved. It is not merely a question of the loss of pay.

Evaluation of Lost Opportunity

Yet another context for the rabbinic employment of the concept of opportunity cost is provided by a controversy between R. Mana and R. Yose, as reported in the Jerusalem Talmud, *Moed Kattan*, II:3. There are two textual versions of this talmudic passage[9] as well as several different interpretations of it.[10] However, it is clear that in this debate the parties are concerned with issues of microeconomic significance. In particular, they are endeavouring to establish the point at which an entrepreneur can be said to have incurred an opportunity cost. One debater emphasizes loss of "profit". The other emphasizes loss of "working capital" as the criterion.

The question here is the circumstances under which local merchants may be permitted to purchase goods from a passing caravan of traders during the intermediate days between holidays. In the discussion, it is assumed that the passing traders are willing to sell their merchandise at prices lower than those pertaining after the holidays. Hence, if the local merchants do not purchase during the intermediate period, they are foregoing a business opportunity.

The passages dealing with the holidays and the caravan include the following:

> [II.A] R. Jacob bar Aha in the name of Rabbis: "Since produce up for sale goes to waste, it is permitted to move it about on the intermediate days of a festival [to keep it fresh]."

---

[8] For a fuller exposition, see, B. Gordon, *The Economic Problem in Biblical and Patristic Thought* (Leiden: Brill, 1989), Ch. I.

[9] For the various interpretations of this passage, see, Dov Ratner, *Ahavat Zion v' Yerushalaim*, Moed Kattan (Vilno, 1911) p. 93.

[10] C.f., *Korban Ha-Edah*. See, in particular, R. David Frankel's Commentary, *Korban Ha-Edah*, T.J. Moed Katan II:3.

B] R. Jacob bar Aha in the name of R. Yose: "In the case of a caravan it is permitted to buy produce from them on the intermediate days of the festival. For people know that a caravan is coming, and so the prices go down [as a consequence of the increased supply of produce that is expected]."
C] Said R. Mana, "If someone knows that if he does not purchase produce from the caravan, his profit will go down, he may purchase from it. If not, he may not do so."
D] Said R. Yose b. R. Bun, "Profit and principal are one and the same. If he knows that if he does not purchase the produce, he will lose his working capital, he may purchase produce on the intermediate days of the festival, and if not, he may not purchase at that time."[11]

For our purposes it is [C] and [D] which are of particular interest.

R. Mana is arguing that a merchant who refrains from purchasing will suffer a cut in his margin of profit, and this cut constitutes a case of foregone opportunity. A smaller profit is tantamount to a loss. The reasoning here may be illustrated as follows. Suppose that the merchant's selling price for the goods in question after the holidays is $115, and that his purchasing price after the holidays is $110. The profit margin is $5. However, suppose further that the "caravan" purchasing price had been $100. If the merchant had purchased during the intermediate period, his profit margin would have been $15. Hence, by refraining from trade with the caravan he has lost $10. The loss of profit provides a ground for allowing merchants to buy in intermediate periods.[12]

R. Yose's position is rather different, and it is somewhat more complex. He directs attention to loss of "working capital" instead of loss of profit as the basis for evaluating opportunity cost. As Yose states: "If he [the merchant] knows that if he does not purchase the produce [from the caravan] he will lose his working capital, he may purchase produce on the intermediate days of the festival . . .".

What does R. Yose mean by "working capital"? A clue to his meaning is provided by his opening statement concerning "profit" and "principal." It would seem that for this scholar, working capital comprises two components ["Agro V'Karno Keren hoo." *M.K.* II:3]. One of the components is "principal" in the sense of the outlay which the merchant makes on the goods in which he is

---

[11] *Talmud Yerushalmi, Moed Kattan* (trans. Jacob Neusner), (Chicago: University of Chicago Press, 1986) p. 164.
[12] The foregoing money sums, it should be emphasized, are purely hypothetical. The rabbis themselves do not spell out their positions by using arithmetical illustrations.

trading.[13] The second component is "profit". Here, Yose appears to be employing the term "profit" in a sense which came to be distinguished in modern microeconomics as "normal profit". This latter is regarded as part of the cost of production for the businessman.

Yose's definition of "profit", it should be emphasized, is different from that of his opponent in debate. R. Mana's analysis of foregone opportunity implies that all profit is a surplus over cost, where cost is understood as the merchant's outlay on the goods in question. In contrast, Yose regards cost as including some profit margin, [the cost of buying, storing or processing the merchandise] as well as the outlay. Yose's approach, it can be remarked, implies that, in business there may be above-normal, or "excess", profit, at times.

Given this difference between the two scholars, it is understandable that their approaches to opportunity cost also differ. Yose's position may be illustrated, as follows. Suppose that the merchant requires a minimum profit margin of 10% on the purchase price of goods in order to maintain his working capital. Further assume (as in the previous illustration in connection with R. Mana) that the purchasing price of goods after the holidays is $110. This means that to avoid a loss of working capital, if he buys after the holidays, Yose's merchant must be able to sell those goods for $121 (i.e., $110 + 10%). However, assume also (as before) that the selling price of the goods after the holidays is only $115. In these circumstances, the merchant has suffered a loss of working capital of $6 (i.e. $121 less $115). It is this $6 which measures the extent of loss incurred by not buying during the intermediate days from the passing caravan.

It can be added that should Yose's merchant have purchased from the caravan, he would have more than merely maintained his working capital. At the caravan purchasing price of $100, the merchant needed to be able to sell at $110 (i.e., $100 + 10%) to avoid capital loss. However, with an assumed selling price of $115 after the holidays, the merchant both maintains working capital and earns an above-normal, or "excess", profit of $5 (i.e. $115 less $110).

The fact that the merchant foregoes this $5 of excess profit by not purchasing from the caravan, it should be emphasized, is not

---

[13] C.f. Marcus Jastrow, *A Dictionary of the Targumim, the Talmud Babli and Yerushalmi, and the Midrashic Literature* (New York: The Judaica Press, 1975), Vol. I, p. 14. Here, Jastrow equates "principal" (in the context of *Y.M. Kat.* II, 81) with "cost-price".

relevant to Yose's calculation of the degree of lost opportunity. The reason for this lack of relevance is that loss of excess profit is not loss of working capital, in his view. Working capital includes normal profit only.

To recapitulate, R. Mana found that it was a loss of *profit* of $10 (i.e., $115 less $105) which justified the merchant's buying in the intermediate period. By contrast R. Yose finds the justification in a loss of *working capital* of $6 (i.e., $121 less $115). Hence, there is a clear division between the two on the question of how foregone opportunity is to be assessed. The division is a further example of the extent to which talmudic debate entered into the substance of certain modern controversies on microeconomic issues.

Calculation of Merchant's Loss at a Selling Price of $115

	Purchase Price	R. Mana		R. Yose	
		Profit	Loss of Profit	Minimum Selling Price to Maintain Working Capital*	Loss of Working Capital
From the Caravan	$100	$15	0	$110	0
After Holidays	$110	$ 5	$10	$121	$6

* Assumes that maintenance of working capital requires 10% mark-up on purchasing price.

A Competitive Market

As the foregoing illustrates, the talmudic probing of the meaning of "cost" extended to extraordinary lengths in terms of what is known concerning analysis in other ancient analytical traditions. A similar observation is warranted with respect to the rabbis' investigations of the workings of competitive markets. This latter is an outstanding feature of the tractate, *Baba Metzia*, (60 a–b) and here the rabbis discuss the question of the competitive devices which can be used legitimately by sellers. They considered both non-price and price competition.

In the opinion of Rabbi Judah, non-price competition is illegitimate. He finds sales promotion aimed at the attraction of customers from other entrepreneurs to be an unfair trade practice. However, this is not the view of the Sages (*Chachamin*). These latter are impressed by the fact that such competition challenges fellow entrepreneurs to follow suit. The Sages are also supportive of price competition. In fact, they consider the practice a "blessing", and they substantiate their view by asserting that price competition is generally healthy because it is instrumental in effecting "an expansion of the market." Rabbi Judah is not impressed by this argument.

The Sages' reference to "an expansion of the market" is taken up by later commentators. These understand the "expansion" to mean a reduction in the unit price of the product at retail. The reduction, they observe further, will lead to concern among wholesalers whose expectations are altered thereby. In the expectation that retail prices will fall even further, the wholesalers will dispose of their stocks. Hence, their expectation becomes self-fulfilling. There is a further reduction in retail price. (ad loc Rashi).

As the discussion of market phenomena proceeds, the talmudic Sages add that in the course of a competitive struggle some sellers may attempt to differentiate their product. For example, they may endeavour to attract customers by means of fancy wrappings or adornments attached to the product. Competitive markets, then, can be subject to degrees of "market imperfection". Here, the rabbis anticipate a line of analysis in modern Economics which only began to come into prominence through the work of Edward Chamberlain and Joan Robinson in the 1920's. These latter, like the talmudic scholars centuries before, realized that there are market conditions which fall between the poles of pristine-pure competition on the one hand, and outright monopoly, on the other.

In general, it is evident that the talmudists depict price formation as occurring through a competitive, communal marketing process. They are careful to emphasize full knowledge as a condition of legitimate market operation. It is stated:

> No bargain may be made over produce before its market-price is known. After its market-price is known a bargain may be made, for even if one dealer has not the produce another will have it . . . A bargain may be made to pay for wares at the cheapest rate that prevails at the time of delivery. Rabbi Judah says: Even if the bargain was not made to pay for wares at the cheapest rate, he may say, 'Give me the wares at such a price, or give me back my money.'[14]

---

[14] *Baba Metzia*, 5:7.

At the same time, it is recognized that certain legitimate transactions can be undertaken despite the absence of full knowledge and a perfect market. These latter are wholesale purchases involving either agricultural products held in stock, e.g. olives in the vat, or products which are intended to serve towards further production. This second category includes "the clayballs of the potter", "lime as soon as the limestone is sunk in the kiln", and manure. Such goods, to use the terminology of the Austrian economist Eugen von Bohm-Bawerk (1851–1914), are "intermediate products" or "social capital".

The rabbis it is clear, are able to make firm analytical distinctions between fixed capital and other articles, between social capital and finished products, and between the competitive market conditions that can be approximated in retailing but less readily in wholesaling.[15] Also notable is the firm definition of what constitutes an exchange transaction. Hence, in the passage quoted above it is the cheapest price *at the time of delivery* which is the relevant rate. This reflects the basic principle that: "All movable goods are legally acquired only by the act of drawing them into the purchaser's possession."[16] In other words, the determining factor in a sale is delivery of the goods concerned to the buyer. Up to that point, any risk of loss or damage to the goods is carried by the seller.[17]

The Role of Demand

Before the advent of neo-classical economic thought, the role of demand in price formation was accorded little analytical regard by major economists. However, the talmudists did not fail to consider this aspect of markets. The most notable occasion for reflection on the significance of demand in the talmudic context was provided by an episode dating from the first century C.E. This episode involved the price of birds used as sacrifices in the Temple in Jerusalem.

According to *Tractate Keritut*: "It came to pass that the price of a couple of birds (frequently used in Jerusalem as the poor man's sacrifice) rose to one gold dinar. (One gold dinar had the exchange value of 25 silver dinarim). As a result of this prohibitive price few people could afford such luxury. So R. Gamaliel vowed not to rest

---

[15] Wholesaling and retailing are also distinguished clearly in *Demai* 2:4.

[16] *Shebiith*, 10:9.

[17] The Talmud also deals with, sales of immovable property (*Kiddushin*, 1:5); disputes over whether or not transfers of goods have occurred (*Shebuoth*, 7:6); and, the relative status of buyer and seller whilst a transaction is in progress (*Baba Bathra*, 5:7–8).

until the price of a pair will be reduced to one silver dinar, that is 1/25 of a gold dinar. In order that this come to pass, he decided to reduce the *demand* for that product. This was facilitated by the Talmudic Academy which ruled that one sacrifice may take the place of the usually required five. The ratio then was 5:1. As a result of this ruling, the demand actually fell and was followed by a spectacular dip in prices. The very same evening a pair could be obtained for a quarter of a silver dinar, that is 1/100 of a gold dinar, by far exceeding R. Gamaliel's expectations."[18]

Here, Rabbi Gamaliel set out to deal with a situation in which demand was strong, but supply relatively inelastic. By altering the quantity demanded at any one price, he demonstrated the role of demand in price formation in a most spectacular fashion. The unexpectedly large fall in price over a very short period indicates a high degree of inelasticity in the short-run supply of birds.

The talmudic scholars also considered the role of demand in their discussion of *Truma* (tithe).[19] Only the priests were allowed to eat *Truma*, so the demand for the tithe (considered as a product) was relatively small and did not fluctuate to any appreciable extent. The scholars observed that the market price of *Truma* was considerably lower than that of the so-called "common" product consumed by the public at large. They attributed the lower price to the fact that the demand of the priests was of a different character from that of the public. Here, the talmudists appear to have approached the concept of the elasticity of demand, although they did not actually employ the term.

---

[18] *Babylonian Talmud, Tractate Keritut*, 1:7.
[19] *Babylonian Talmud, Tractate Baba Mezia*, p. 38a, and Rashi, *San.* 26a.

CHAPTER SIX
GAME THEORY—THE TALMUDIC MINIMAX

The purpose of this chapter is to demonstrate that within the purview of the Talmudic dialectics, the game method was often utilized to solve intricate questions, theoretical as well as practical. This is particularly evident in Talmudic discussions of transactional issues involving conflicting business interests, where complicated decisions have to be made under conditions of uncertainty. In the course of those discussions, the scholars reason in categories which are similar to some of those employed in modern Game Theory.

Games as such, whether of chance or of strategy (upon which game theory is based), have been practiced since time immemorial, including among the ancient Hebrews.[1] The Talmudic scholars were familiar with their characteristics, and they also utilized games of strategy tactics both in their scholarly discourses and in their solving of transactional disputes. The historical background, methodological process, and approach to the solution of conflict situations in the Talmud combined to promote employment of game method in the quest for the solution of certain economic problems.

The Minimax Principle

Game theory is one of the youngest contributions to modern economic analysis. It is a theory of conflict situations that likens economic behaviour to games of strategy, such as poker, chess and even war. The modern origins of the theory may be traced to the second decade of the present century, but it was only clearly established as a scientific discipline through the publication, in 1944, of the *Theory of Games and Economic Behaviour* by John Von Neumann and Oskar Morgenstern.[2] In essence, game theory is concerned with competitive economic behaviour, and as in a real game, it is characterized by the presence of common factors, such as conflicting interests, incomplete information, and the interplay of rational decisions

---

[1] Consult "Games", *Encyclopedia Judaica* (Jerusalem: Keter, 1971) Vol. 7, pp. 303–4, and "Gambling", ibid., pp. 299–303.
[2] J. von Neumann and O. Morgenstern, *Theory of Games and Economic Behaviour* (Princeton: Princeton University Press, 1944).

under conditions of uncertainty. This, in turn, subjects the decision maker to certain risks. Game theory may, therefore, help the risk-taker to select an optimum strategy.[3]

For our purpose, it will suffice to mention that the basic tool of game theory is a payoff *matrix* with alternative choices or strategies for parties involved in a conflict of interests, in which the actions of one party influences its rival. For example, A&B, two opponents, are pursuing their self-interest. Seen from A's perspective, if he is to succeed, he must try to guess how his moves will be countered by his rival. To put this colloquially: "what does he think I think he will do?" A wrong guess might prove too costly. How is the game resolved? The simplest way is to list the *worst* possible result that an opponent could inflict, and find the strategies that realize the *best* outcome from the list.

Thus, in a contest between A and B, A will pursue a strategy of maximizing the minimum gain, (abbr. max-min), while B will attempt to minimize his maximum loss (abbr. min-max). The optimum strategy (or mix of strategies) is then determined by the so called minimax principle. Although game theory is too complex for full scale analysis of real world cases, many can be examined in simplified or miniature form, particularly when applied to simple business situations.

Background to the Talmudic Game Method

In order to prepare the ground for the discussion of the talmudic game method, it is relevant to note both something of the historical background and the methodological approach which characterizes the talmudic debate.

Historically, games of chance were well known to the ancient world. In fact, some oriental gambling games go back as far as 2100 B.C.E. The Lydians, Herodotus relates, were adept in the invention of games. And gambling with dice was particularly fashionable at the Persian court during the reign of Cyrus the Young, at the end of the 5th century B.C.E. As for the "early tribes of Germany", Tacitus writes, they, "make games of hazard a serious occupation

---

[3] A recent discussion is, Mohammed Dore et al. (eds.), *John Von Neumann and Modern Economics* (Oxford: Clarendon, 1989), pp. 151–62. See in particular, *Thinking Strategically*, by Avinash Dixit and Barry Nalebuff (W.W. Norton & Co., New York-London, 1991) It is an interesting popularly written book. For an excellent review of this subject, see Andrew Schotter & Gerhard Schwodiauer, "Economics and Game Theory: A Survey", *Journal of Economic Literature*, (June 1980 Vol. XVIII, No. 2) pp. 479–527.

even when sober . . .", while in less sober moments they even
gambled themselves into slavery.[4] The ancient Hebrews, too, were
acquainted with gambling. There is ample reference to guessing
games in the Bible (Judg. 14:12 ff; 1 Kings 10:1–3). However, it
was from the Mishnaic times onward that the rabbis described
gambling as a form of robbery. As for the characteristics of the
talmudic game method, three motifs distinguish the talmudic debate: the transactional, the strategic and the playful.

The Transactional Motif

Historically, the transactional motif has its origin in the early
annals of Talmudic literature. Thus, in the Midrashic volume *Sifrai*
(32:25), which dates back to ca. 200 CE., the term *Nosse V'noten*
("give and take") is used to designate scholarly controversies. And
in the Talmud the two synonymous expressions *Masso Umatan* and
Nosse V'noten are applied idiomatically to ordinary business dealings
like "buying and selling." The Aramaic equivalent for "nosse
V'noten" is *Shakla V'taria*, meaning "give and take."[5] These terms
were probably derived from the barter practice prevalent in antiquity.
    Characteristically, those transactional expressions were used in-
terchangeably in Talmudic parlance, both for business dealings
and scholarly discourse. Nowadays, too, we speak of "selling an
idea." And in the contemporary State of Israel, the term *Masso
U'matan* is frequently employed to describe intricate diplomatic
negotiations.
    In view of the common historical origin and characteristics of
those terms, as well as of their frequent usage both among the
ancients and moderns alike, it is evident that the transactional
motif was an important feature of the talmudic analytical thought
process and, as we shall show, of practical application.

The Strategic Motif

The strategic metaphor figures prominently in talmudic parlance.
Military terms were frequently employed to describe the animated
debates among the scholars. The ingenious arguments and rebut-
tals, the sharp moves and counter moves, the paradigms, the

---

    [4] *Encyclopedia Britannica*, Vol. 9, pp. 1119–21 offers further detail.
    [5] Yoma, 86a, Shabbat 120a, Tossefta, Gittin, V:1, Baba Kama 72a, Sotah 7b,
and in many other places.

questions and methods, were often portrayed in the Talmud as if they took place in a war zone on the battlefield.

Even before the Amoraic period (ca. 200 CE.), the Rabbis referred to those debates in military terms. Inasmush as sharpness, lucidity and precision were central in their discussions, the scholars used the military metaphore to highlight the virtues of the battles of the mind. They referred to them as *Mithamtah-shel-Torah*, "the war for the sake of the Torah". It was a.o., a battle for clarity and understanding. (Sanh. 111b).

Indeed, there are many references in the Talmud to this effect. Suffice it to mention that the Rabbis interpreted Biblical verses which glorify military prowess as referring to the battles of the mind. (Kidd. 30b). For example, the Biblical verse in I Samuel, 16:18, in which David's qualities are praised, is interpreted by R. Judah in the name of Rav (3rd. cent. C.E.) as follows: . . . *that is cunning in playing*—"knowing the right questions to ask"; *a mighty valiant man;*—"knowing the correct answers"; *a man of war;*—"knowing how to 'give and take' in the battles of the Torah"; *prudent in matters;*—knowing how to deduce one thing from another"; *and comely person;*—"who demonstrates the proofs for his opinions"; *and the Lord is with him;*—"the ruling is always in accordance with his views." (Ber. 93b).[6]

As can be seen the leitmotif of these interpretations is that warfare and debate have strategic similarities, and that in the war of ideas "strategic depth" is the name of the game.

The Playful Motif

An interesting feature of this intellectual duel is that the discussions among the scholars were frequently gamelike. The debaters, like seasoned players, were out looking and trying to one-up each other in a clash of wits, to test the opponent's acumen. This gamelike method was purposely cultivated, in order to elicit twinkles of insight and flashes of brilliance. As the Talmud puts it: *Lehaded bo et Ha-Talmidim*—"to sharpen the intellect of the disciples" (Megillah 15b.)

In fact, the Talmud relates on numerous occasions, that the great Masters purposely used faulty reasoning, in order to test their disciples' keenness of mind. They wanted to know whether they

---

[6] See, Louis Jacobs, *The Talmudic Argument* (Cambridge University Press, 1984), p. 8–11.

would be sufficiently alert to spot mistakes.[7] And since a brisk scholarly mind was called *HARIF*—"sharp", they expressed their preference by quoting the following proverb: . . . "one grain of sharp (harif) pepper is worth more than a bucket full of pump-kins . . ." (Megillah 7a.) The *harif* was extolled because of his brilliance to resolve difficulties and his ability to solve problems.

In light of these motifs, it becomes apparent how the talmudic sages came to extend this threefold method to all sorts of problem solving, especially when dealing with complicated questions of economic conflict.

Kubbiyah—A Zero-Sum Game

Games of strategy as well as of chance are frequently the object of discussion in the Talmud. Among the various games mentioned by the Rabbis is a form of dice called *Kubbiyah*. Its name is derived from the Greek *Kybeia*, meaning cube. It consists of small wooden, mostly painted, cubes and used in games of dice. Inasmuch as in dice the outcome depends entirely on chance and cannot be affected by the cleverness of the players, it is deemed a game of pure chance. The Rabbis characterize *Kubbiyah* as a gambling game where one man's loss is another's gain. Today, such games are classified as a *zero-sum* game because the winnings are just offset by the losses, and like in roulette on an unbiased wheel there is no "system" for playing dice.[8]

Although there is no system in such games, they are not com-pletely devoid of some strategic elements. For instance, amateurs who gamble for fun might resort to a *randomized* strategy. Thus, in a coin-matching play, they can agree to flip the coin X number of times for a game sequence, with each choosing heads and tails half the time. In this way, they can hope, according to the law of probability, to break even. The same goes for the roulette wheel as well as for dice. Still, here no one can *individually* affect the outcome of the game, unless the dice are loaded.

It is interesting to note that the Talmud (Sanh. 24b–25a) makes a distinction between the social status of the "professional gam-bler" and of the amateur who derives his livelihood from another profession. Whereas the former is categorized as a "robber", the

---

[7] See, Taan. 7a, Nazir, 59b, Zev. 13a, Hulin, 43b, Nidda 4b, and other places.

[8] See, Sanh. 24b, along with Rashi's explanation, loc. cit. Note: in describing the various categories of games, we are concerned here only with their characteris-tics for purposes of illustration, and as a point of departure for further analysis.

latter is viewed by the Sages more benignly. The rationale for their opposition toward professional gamblers is explained in socio-economic terms of *Yishuv ha'Olam*, i.e., as being detrimental to "social welfare". Thus, if we should apply the game theory criteria to the talmudic distinction between different categories of gamblers, we may find another reason for the more lenient attitude toward amateur players than to professional gamblers. The former who mostly play for fun may randomize the game to break even, while the latter are always out to "make a killing."

However, games such as chess and poker in which the players can utilize ingenuity to affect the outcome, are in the category of strategic games. The essential difference between games of strategy and games of (pure) chance—according to McKinsey—"lies in the circumstances that intelligence and skill are useful in playing the former but not the latter."[9]

Here, we shall concern ourselves with games of strategy. We shall present two typical examples—the *Asmakhta*, and the highly sophisticated talmudic minimax, called *Pesharah*. They illustrate conflicting business situations in which strategic calculations are of central importance to the outcome of the business venture.

Asmakhta: A Positive-Sum Game

One way of understanding economic activity is to think of it as a game initially involving two single participants, like buyer and seller, producer and consumer, or, lender and borrower. Such exchanges are usually termed *positive-sum* games, because both parties expect positive gains from a given transaction. The talmudic *Asmakhta* meets those criteria.

What is an *Asmakhta*? It is a legal concept with economic ramifications. Generally, it pertains to a business deal between two parties based on a promise but lacking in complete resolve or firm commitment. For example, A pays a portion of his indebtedness to B, leaving the bill of debt with C as a security, and agreeing to pay the *full amount* on the bill if, at a stipulated time, he should fail to pay the balance. This transaction includes two obligations; one relating to the outstanding balance; the second, to the payment of the penalty. (B. B. 168a)

Temporarily, we will ignore the legal question of whether or not such a promise constitutes a firm resolve on the part of A, and

---

[9] J.C.C. McKinsey, *Introduction to the Theory of Games* (New York: McGraw-Hill, 1952), pp. 1–5 ff.

under what circumstances an Asmakhta does or does not confer title[10] for our concern is mainly with the conflicting nature of the problem: its "strategic" significance and analytical relevance. Accordingly, here is a two party bargaining situation in which both participants expect a positive gain from this transaction. The borrower expects to use the loan productively, make a profit, and repay the loan in due time. Whereas the lender, with the collateral on deposit, might calculate that in the event the borrower will not meet the deadline, he will forfeit the *full amount* of the bill, in addition to the portion already paid. Clearly, there are here both risks and opportunities for both of the parties involved. But, that is not all. Suppose the borrower, for whatever reason, becomes destitute or ill. This might well cause additional risks and complications (See Ned. 27b), and require additional precautionary measures as well as careful strategic planning.

In this instance, we have an example of a conflict situation in which the outcome is controlled partly by one side and partly by the opposite side. It is one of many *Asmakhtot* discussed in the Talmud which illustrates the fact that, even in such a simple "positive-sum" game, a proper strategy must be selected for the purpose of minimizing the losses and maximizing the gains. What is the consensus of the sages concerning an *Asmakhta*? The consensus is that an *Asmakhta* does not confer title. The reasoning here is that when one of the parties binds himself to an exaggerated penalty, it indicates a lack of "perfect intention" on the part of that person. As summarized by Marcus Jastrow, "It gives the claimant no rights, because the law presumes that he who made such a promise could not have meant it seriously, but had in view only to give the transaction the character of good faith and solemnity."[11]

The consensus of the Sages, it must be emphasized, cannot be construed as providing an *economic* solution to what was a legally defective business deal in its foundations. Further, in the above example *Asmakhta* is merely illustrative of a positive-sum game, and does not enter into the technical elements of game theory. It is notable however, because of the direction it indicates. More directly relevant, in terms of game theory, is the rabbinic concern with *Pesharah*.

---

[10] For a discussion of this subject, see B. Bathra, 168a, B. Metz, 66a, Ned. 27b, along with the various commentaries and Codes.

[11] *Dictionary of Talmudic and Midrashic Literature*, p. 94.

The Talmudic Minimax: Pesharah

In the course of daily events, people may encounter personal or business situations of a conflicting nature for which the law makes no provision. Sometimes the situation is so entangled, that even the law may find it difficult to disentangle. When in such a predicament, it is prudent to resort to a compromise.

The Rabbis examined such conflict situations analytically and suggested a rational strategy for their resolution by means of *Pesharah*. The term *Pesharah*, as used by the *Tannaim*, denotes compromise or concilliation as well as arbitration. As an illustration, they used relevant models which show that the most prudent way to resolve such conflicts is through a strategic compromise.

Accordingly, the Mishnah in *Ketubot* X:6 discusses three typical conflict situations which necessitate a policy of strategic rationality. For a pointed example we shall select one of those models which illustrate its gamelike nature and solution.

A Creditor's Dilemma

Creditor A has a claim of $100 on debtor B, (who pledged his two fields as security for his debt.) B then sells both fields consecutively, one to C for $50 and the other to D for $50. Thereupon Creditor A gives purchaser D a written declaration: 'I waive any right or claim I have against you'. Creditor A may then distrain upon purchaser C (because of his lien on the field), and C may now distrain on D (since there is a *joint* lien on both fields), and Creditor A may again distrain upon C, while D may now distrain upon A (since A waived any claim against D), and so on, *ad infinitum*, until they cooperatively make a *Pesharah*.[12]

The following chart illustrates one round of consecutive strategic moves in this unending game. The numbers indicate the sequence.

A close examination of this entangled transaction reveals its strategic nature and purpose. What would have happened had A not waived his claim against D? Then, A could have distrained upon D, because as the second purchaser, he is legally on the first firing-line. A could then proceed and do the same to C, and the process would have ended here and now. But this might have been "unfair" to D and C. True, they should have checked with the court registry regarding the legal status of those fields before they

---

[12] In this quotation the authors have designated the money sums in terms of dollars for the sake of clearer explication of the dilemma.

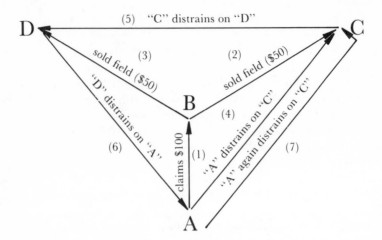

purchased them. This notwithstanding, they have a moral claim that their transaction was in "good faith".

Assuming that ". . . most people like to be treated fairly, and like to treat others fairly"—as Richard H. Thaler concludes[13]—A is faced with a dilemma; he must choose between selfishness and sensible cooperation. Instead, and apparently for his own reasons, A decided to let D off the hook and embarked on the risky business of gamesmanship, resulting in a vicious cycle of musical chairs, with one player always remaining as if in suspended animation.

Let us see how. As we have seen with A's renunciation of the claim against D, A takes away the field from C. As a result D and A have each a field; C is out. Again, when C takes away the field from D, C and A have the fields and D is out. Then, when A takes away again the field from C, A has both fields and both C and D are temporarily out until D takes it back from A and C is out. At this point in the game they are ready for a second round, and so it goes until they agree to adjust their claims by mutual concessions. Such a compromise, it can be observed, is far removed from the behaviour analyzed in the standard game theoretic model, but the talmudic discussion continues beyond this.

Collusion versus Collision

It must be pointed out that there are still other strategic moves that can take place in this game. For example, suppose purchaser D, a

[13] Richard H. Thaler, "Anomalies—the Ultimatum Game", *The Journal of Economic Perspectives*, Vol. 2, (Fall 1988), pp. 195–206.

seasoned player, decides to collude with C against A. Specifically, D intimates to C as follows: "If you distrain on me, A will certainly distrain on you. Therefore, let's make a deal, I will pay you an X amount and do not touch my field", or still better, "Sell to me the field you hold for $25 or $30 and your pay-off will be more then in any eventual compromise." Should that happen, D will now have both fields, and A, since he renounced any claim on D, will be left high and dry, without any field. (See, *Tosaphot* RID, loc. cit.)

However, chances are that D would not embark on such an "unfair" venture, if only on account of his gratitude for A's releasing him from his obligation. A seems to have been clever enough to let D off the hook to gain his good will. And now, with neither collusion nor collision by either party, the only solution to end this vicious cycle, is to reach a *Pesharah*.

Still two questions remain. What happened to B who is the real culprit in this affair? Afterall, it was he who sold the pledged fields illegally. Second, what could have been A's motive for waiving his claim against D?

Regarding B's illegal transaction, he is deemed to be either dead, or that the debt is uncollectable. Thus, for all practical intents and purposes B is out of the picture. As for A's motives, in the absence of an obvious lead from the text of the *Talmud*, it could be assumed that A might have suspected that if he distrained on both C and D these two together might be powerful enough to retaliate and cause him other business losses. Thus, A might have won the battle but would have lost the war. Another concern of A's might have been that C and D have some moral claim in that their transactions were made in "good faith." Sensing trouble, and to avoid possible complications, A made a premeditated move of "good will" to oblige D in his actions. The Talmud describes a deed of this nature as *Shtar Passais*, a "writ of good will" (B.B. 154b). An element of "fairness", too, might have been part of this strategy.[14] Be that as it may, it was this skillful move that lead in a roundabout way to an optimal solution.

And now that all chips are in and all are forced into a compromise, how is this game likely to be resolved? If the solution is to be based on strategic cooperation, A would settle for 50% of the debt, and C and D will receive 25% each. Result—A will get the

---

[14] It can be added that other factors involved in "distraining" may include the transaction costs (e.g., legal fees, loss of time, and psychological stress). These, and other considerations, give the parties incentives to seek a co-operative solution.

maximum of the minimum, and C and D will receive the minimum of the maximum. It is an equilibrium that is distinctly positive.

Let us now see who gains and who loses. Off-hand, it would seem that all three lose. But upon further consideration all somehow benefited by this cooperation. A emerged practically unscathed because he had waived his claim of 50% in the first place. Thus, A has his 50% plus his desired good will from D, which, to him, might be a priceless payoff. Again, C, and D could have lost everything, since they have purchased the fields upon which there was a joint lien. Their transaction was, to begin with, illegal. Now the game is resolved satisfactorily via the Talmudic minimax called *Pesharah*.

In sum, in this intricate situation, cooperation replaces combat, "fairness" takes precedence over "gamesmanship", and in place of either collision or collusion they become "sensible cooperators." Here it should be noted that the classical example which proves that very point is provided by L.B. Lave in his essay on the Prisoners' Dilemma Game.[15]

Without going into details, in this game two suspects are interrogated separately and faced with alternative potential sentences, depending on whether (a) one confesses, (b) neither of them confess or (c) both confess. After considering the advantages and pitfalls of various strategies, the suspects will find that confession is the dominant strategy. Although from the suspects' point of view, by not confessing they could be made better off, this can only happen if they do so jointly, which is impossible without communication.

Of course, no analogy is perfect. Nonetheless, in both scenarios, cooperation is the dominant strategy. In both, the prisoners' and creditors' dilemma, the subjects behaved in accordance with game theory. By exercising strategic rationality, they resolved a conflict situation through sensible cooperation. While in game theory it is the minimax, in the Talmud the name of the game is *Pesharah*.[16]

A Pay-off Matrix

The principle behind the *creditor's dilemma*, just as the *prisoner's dilemma*, illustrates the tension between a "tit for tat" strategy and

---

[15] L.B. Lave, "An Empirical Approach to the Prisoners' Dilemma Game", *Quarterly Journal of Economics*, Vol. 75, (August 1962), pp. 424–436.

[16] See also, T. Jerus. *Kethuboth* 60b, in which the advantages of *Pesharah* are discussed and illustrated.

collusive cooperation. Let us look at the outcome of the various strategies.

1. If A "defects" and distrains on both C and D, A gets $100 and his opponents (C and D) get 0.
2. If D and C "defect" and conspire against A, both D and C will get $100 (D gets $70 and C $30) and A gets 0.
3. If A renounces his claim against D and distrains on C, a strategy of "tit for tat" emerges, where one does to his opponent what the opponent has just done to him. As a result the money will move from hand to hand in a clockwise direction in a complete circuit, with more rounds to follow.
4. If the parties agree on a cooperative strategy, all participants will benefit from this sensible course of action.

The following diagram illustrates the various strategies and outcomes. The payoff matrix is presented from A's point of view, who, as in a chess or poker game, must try to guess his opponents' moves and countermoves, bluffs and counterbluffs, as many moves ahead as possible.

IF / AND IF	A cooperates	A defects
C & D cooperate	A gets 50	A gets 100
	opponents get 50	opponents get 0
C & D defect	A gets 0	
	C & D get 100	

Explanation of the Diagram

Without knowing what C and D will do, A must decide whether to "cooperate" or to "defect". If all cooperate the combined gains are optimal (50 + 50 = 100). However, there are strong incentives to defect. If A assumes that C and D will cooperate, he would gain by defecting (distrain on both) because it will double the amount (100). If he assumes that C and D will defect he will find that it is in his interest to absolve D of his debt because that strategy enables him to stay in the game and distrain on C instead of receiving 0. Although this strategy leads to mutual defection, he nevertheless calculates that the "merry go round" tactic must ultimately end in cooperative behaviour.

Some games of course, have a structure that makes it impossible to use a payoff matrix as in a two player's game. Inasmuch as in this model of the "creditor's dilemma" there are three players (A, C and D), in the case of mutual defection, it is impossible to use a conventional payoff matrix without becoming bogged down in a swamp of mathematical complications. We have, therefore, chosen the three sector circular figure to illustrate the circuitous quality of this part of the game. The money moves clockwise.

Although the usual payoff matrix can become complicated, other matrices can be used to help simplify matters. In the previous example, it is possible to set up a matrix as follows: The columns correspond to the players A, C and D, the rows will indicate each transaction.

For example, when all cooperate, the following matrix can be used to describe this situation

A	C	D
0	50	50
50	25	25

The top row represents the beginning transaction in which C and D have fields worth 50 each. The second row shows that as a result of mutual cooperation, C and D end up with 25 each and A would end up with 50. Note also the entire process can be described by a matrix with two rows.

In the case in which A defects and C and D cooperate (acquiesce), the following matrix summarizes the transactions that transpire. This matrix also has two rows.

A	C	D
0	50	50
100	0	0

The simplest case to describe mathematically is when C and D defect and A cooperates (acquiesces). This matrix uses only one row.

A	C	D
0	50	50

The most interesting case mathematically is the instance where A suspects that C and D will defect and therefore absolves D which results in mutual defection.

A	C	D
0	50	50
50	0	50
50	50	0
100	0	0
50	0	50
50	50	0
100	0	0
50	0	50
50	50	0
100	0	0

This matrix continues on repeating the pattern of the second, third and fourth rows, until the strategy changes. This means the number of rows in the final matrix will be much greater than in any of the other cases.

In sum, whereas in this method, the addition of two or more players, for instance, would not matter (since it would merely increase the number of columns by two), it would be impossible to do the same in a conventional payoff matrix. Instead, the several players would have to be combined to form a 2×2 payoff matrix, as in the case of the "creditor's dilemma".

Summary and Conclusion

We have embarked on a brief historical and analytical journey to examine the intellectual setting of the talmudic Sages in which the game method plays a pivotal part. In discussing the three kinds of motifs as well as the zero-sum game of *Kubbiyah*, we endeavored to show that the Rabbis were in a position to use their familiarity with the characteristics of such games, as well as with the game method, so as to extend the same to all sorts of problem solving, including questions of economic conflict situations. And by focusing on the *Asmakhta* phenomenon, as an example of a positive-sum game, the ground was prepared for the presentation of the sophisticated talmudic minimax, the *Pesharah*.

This last, it should be emphasized, is a particularly interesting line of analysis in that it is focused on a group of individuals who exhibit *Complete interdependence*, i.e., every (possible) action of any member affects the satisfaction of every other member. This situation may be distinguished from that of *Complete independence*, where no (possible) action of any member of the group can influence the satisfaction of any other member, and from *One-way dependence*, where every (possible) action of at least one member affects the satisfaction of another member or other members but no other member can affect his satisfaction.[17] In *Pesharah*, then, we encounter explicit emphasis on the interdependence of economic agents. Such emphasis, it is widely claimed, is a hallmark of the game theory contribution to modern economic thought.

Finally, there is the issue of the convergence of economics and ethics. It is the consensus among the talmudic Sages that economic conflicts are best resolved by means of *Bitzzu'a*. (*Bitzzu'a* is a term synonymous with and equivalent to *Pesharah*.) They consider a friendly compromise as a "judgement of peace." Thus, R. Joshua b. Korhah states that, "Bitzzu'a is a meritorious act". He bases it on the Scriptual injunction: "Execute judgment of truth and peace in your gates" (Zech. 8:16), commenting, that justice which involved both peace and charity was to be found in *Bitzzu'a*.[18]

This method of settling economic conflicts is considered to be particularly advantageous because it rests on voluntariness, mutual consent and sensible cooperation. *Pesharah*, then, is an economic-problem solving method in which strategic rationality, prudence and ethics are remarkably interwined.[19] Thus, not only may *Pesharah* qualify as a proto game theory but also serve as an object lesson in matters of economics and ethics.

---

[17] On these three, group situations, consult, Clem Tisdell, "Some Bounds Upon the Pareto Optimality of Group Behaviour," *Kyklos*, Vol. XIX (1966), pp. 81–105. Tisdell observes (p. 84) that the complete interdependence case is the most interesting, "since it more closely approximates the conditions of our own society . . .".

[18] Siphrei Deut. 17; Tos. Sanh. 1:2–3; Sanh. 6b; T. Jerus. Sanh. 1:1, 18b.

[19] Game theory too can be employed in the elucidation of ethical issues. Consult, e.g., John R. Chamberlin, "Ethics and Game Theory", *Ethics and International Affairs*, Vol. 3 (1989), pp. 261–76.

CHAPTER SEVEN

RISK, UNCERTAINTY AND EXPECTATION

In any environment which allows for individual and group enterprise, some degree of risk, as well as some elements of uncertainty and expectation, will be features of virtually every human endeavour. If these three decision-making categories are common to human effort in general, it can be observed that they possess special relevance where business enterprise is concerned.

The psychological component permeates all three categories of decision-making. In business life, this component manifests itself in feelings of both faith and doubt concerning the outcome of a particular undertaking. Subjective reflection on the possibilities of the undertaking's success or failure are constant conscious or subconscious companions to the activity of conducting a business venture.

Economists have sought to establish objective analyses of the three categories, distinguishing both the qualitative features and the quantitative dimensions of risk, uncertainty and expectation. In modern economics these concepts have been subjected to rigorous theoretical scrutiny as well as empirical investigation of their incidence and relevance in economic life. These investigations have generated a substantial body of literature dealing with the issues involved.[1]

Analysis of risk, uncertainty and expectation is also a feature of talmudic literature, and in this chapter we explore that analysis in the light of modern economics. Each of the three categories is examined in turn, first with reference to modern understandings of what they imply, and then with reference to the talmudic treatments of the same phenomenon.

Risk and Probability

"Risk" is a familiar term with many meanings, connotations and functions. Among others, it implies a gamble and danger,

---

[1] Recent contributions include, Sean Holly and Andrew H. Hallet, *Optimal Control, Expectation and Uncertainty* (New York: Cambridge University Press, 1989); and Peter Diamond and Michael Rothschild, *Uncertainty in Economics* (San Diego: Academic Press, 1989). A pioneering study is, Frank H. Knight, *Risk, Uncertainty and Profit* (New York: Harper and Row, 1921).

speculation and the possibility of loss, venture and peril. Whenever one makes a decision, but is unable to anticipate the outcome with certainty, there is an element of risk. Almost every situation involves some element of chance, no matter how slight. Games of chance, for instance, provide us with prime examples of situation involving risk.

A distinguishing feature of risk is its susceptibility to measurement or probability distribution. The degree of risk can be quantified and, in that sense, it is predictable. For example, a return on an investment may be said to be "risky" in that it has a one to ten chance (0.1 probability) of resulting in a loss, that it has a four to five in ten chances of attaining a particular value, or that it is subject to some other distribution. Since there is an element of predictability respecting the possibility of gain or loss, "risk" may be defined as the likelihood of an event for which a probability can be reasonably estimated.

Probability, it should be added, can be viewed in either objective or subjective terms. In a game of dice, for example, the objective view holds, since the outcomes do not depend on the judgement of the players. This is not the case in the world of business, since an investment is usually motivated by some "degree of belief" on the part of the investor. Here, probability must be viewed in subjective terms. The psychological make-up of the individual risk-taker cannot be ignored, because the attitude toward risk will vary with that make-up.

The Risk Factor in the Talmud

As we have seen in earlier chapters, the Talmud approaches juridical questions by means of a "case method" rather than a "principles method". This holds for the treatment of business relations in general, and for the examination of business risks, in particular. There are many talmudic discussions involving such risks, and one of these is contained in the Tractate *Kethuboth*. This Tractate deals with, among other matters, the characteristics of a marriage contract called *Kethubah*. The framework for the debate is the content of a marriage document, but this provides an occasion for far-reaching economic analysis of risk and related issues.

The *Kethubah* is a marriage deed in which the duties of a husband to his wife are recorded. The deed contained, in addition to a variety of other requirements, provision for a settlement of a certain sum which is due to the wife in the event that she becomes widowed or divorced. It was also the custom that a wife brought a dowry to her husband upon marriage, and during the talmudic period it became the institutionalized norm that the husband, in return for the dowry, was obliged to add a corresponding amount to his wife's *Kethubah*, i.e. to the settlement she could expect if widowed or divorced.

The actual amount which the husband must add was held to depend, in part, on the degree of liquidity of the assets which comprised the dowry. Those assets might consist of "ready money", highly liquid gold instruments such as gold *denarii*, easily redeemable merchandise, or objects of "estimated value" like gold bars or utensils. The various degrees of liquidity which might be attached to different assets evoked considerable debate, and it was held that if the dowry was in the form of ready cash or highly liquid "near money", the husband was required to augment his wife's *Kethubah* to the extent of fifty percent more than the value of the dowry.[2] The Jerusalem Talmud offers an explicitly economic-rational ground for this latter provision. The fifty percent more is warranted by the fact that the husband is in a position to invest the funds from the dowry and thereby derive a profit from them throughout his life.[3]

There are two Mishnaic passages which bear directly on the foregoing provision. The first of these reads:

> . . . If a woman undertook to bring to her husband (on marriage) one thousand *denarii*, he must assign to her (as her *Kethubah*) a corresponding sum of fifteen *Maneh* . . . (a *Maneh* = 100 *denarii*, so fifteen *Maneh* = 1,500 *denarii*).[4]

The second passage embodies the same principle, although the sums of money employed for purposes of illustration are much smaller. It reads:

> . . . If a woman undertook to bring to her husband (on marriage) ready money, every *Sela* (a *Sela* = 4 *denarii*) of hers counts as six *denarii* . . . (i.e., fifty percent is added to the amount the woman brings, as in the case of ready money in the first passage).[5]

When confronted with the above passages, the talmudic Rabbis were intrigued as to why it was necessary to have two Mishnaic

---

[2] For the discussion of the various degrees of liquidity, see *Kethuboth*, 67a. In this discussion, the contributors develop categories which suggest analogies with those adopted in modern monetary thought (M_1, M_2, etc.).

[3] See, T. Jerusalem, Tractate *Kethuboth*, Chapter 6:40a.

[4] Babylonian Talmud, *Kethuboth*, Chapter 6:66a. The citations are from the English translation of the Babylonian Talmud, Soncino Press, London.

[5] ibid., p. 66b.

clauses to state the same principle concerning the added fifty
percent. In their discussion, the Rabbis considered the necessity of
the twofold statement from the viewpoint that the capital sum
might yield profit. They also considered that necessity from the
viewpoint that a loss might be incurred. It is in this latter context
that the factor of risk emerges explicitly as an element in their
reasoning.

The Profit Dimension

The reason for the twofold statement is explained in the *Gemara*, as
follows:

> . . . He taught first about a major transaction (1,000 denarii) and
> then taught about a minor transaction (in the second Mishnah). And
> (both rulings were) necessary. For had the major transaction only
> been taught, it might have been assumed (that it applied to this only)
> because the profit (it brings in) is large but not to a minor transac-
> tion, the profit from which is small (hence it was) necessary (to state
> the latter.)[6]

In this explanation, the case of a "major investment" of 1,000
denarii, with the probability of a "large profit", is distinguished
from that of a "minor investment" of 4 *denarii*, with the probability
of only a "minor profit". It is held that both *Mishnot* (plural of
Mishnah) were necessary to emphasize that the husband is subject
to the same rule with respect to the extra sum he must add to his
wife's *Kethubah* regardless of the magnitudes of that sum and the
profits resulting.

The explanation is notable for its demonstration of the extent to
which the talmudic Sages were ready to incorporate categories such
as "capital investment" and "profit" in their reasoning on juridical
issues. It is clear that it is precisely on account of the possibility of
the emergence of profit from a capital investment that the Rabbis
were constrained to impose upon the husband an additional payment to his wife's *Kethubah*. The payment might be construed (to
use a modern phrase) as a form of interest payment for the use of
loanable funds. However, this construction is not valid.[7]

---

[6] ibid.

[7] See, *Mordekhai* The Commentary on Kethuboth, by Mordekhai ben Hillel
(13th century), loc. cit. He quotes his contemporary R. Samuel b. Barukh as
follows: " . . . yet this is not to be viewed as interest, since, even if the husband
divorced his wife soon thereafter, he would still have to add one third (to her
Kethubah.) But a regular loan is (usually) extended for a lengthy period and the
return therefrom is in the category of *Agar Natar*—a' compensation for waiting."

The Loss Dimension

The Talmud offers a second explanation of the need for the two Mishnah's on this subject. Instead of stressing the profit which may be associated with use of a wife's dowry, this second explanation directs attention to the possibility of loss. The key term here is *Zeyoona*, a term which refers to the presence of business risk and the potential for losses in business.[8] The relevance of *Zeyoona* is emphasized in the continuation of the *Gemara* cited above. This continuation considers why it was necessary for the earlier scholars to include the first Mishnah (dealing with the higher value dowry) given that the second Mishnah appears to be stating the same general rule. The continuation reads:

> . . . And had we have been informed of that of the minor transaction, it might have been said (to apply to this only) because the *Zeyoona* is small but not to a large transaction where the *Zeyoona* is great (hence it was) necessary (to state the former).[9]

Here, it is recognised that business investment is fraught with risk, and the bigger the capital investment, the bigger the potential for loss. When a huge sum, such as 1,000 *denarii*, is turned into risk capital the stakes are high. As Adin Steinsaltz observes, here, there are "strong possibilities of loss and great risks."[10] There is the temptation, in the face of substantial loss, to deny the wife her due *Kethubah*. However, the Talmud does not allow the unsuccessful,

---

(B. Metz. 63 b). (Freely translated by the authors from the original text.) We might add that the above is not the last word in this debate.

Incidentally, some 1500 years later, Alfred Marshall (1840–1924), the distinguished English economist, used the same talmudic designation in order to mitigate the irksomeness of Senior's abstinence theory of interest. He substituted the term "waiting" for "abstinence", i.e., that interest is a compensation for "waiting."

[8] See, Alexander Kohut, *Aruch Completum* (in Hebrew), (Pardes Publishing House, 1955), p. 287. The author translates the term *Zeyan* as "losses", citing other talmudic sources such as *Menahot* 77a, and *Baba Bathra* 90a to this effect. Kohut expressly prefers this understanding to Rashi's description of *Zeyoona* as "expenditures and responsibility". See also, in particular, Marcus Jastrow, *Dictionary of Talmud Bavli* (Pardes Publishing House, 1950), p. 392. Jastrow understands the term *Zeyoona* to mean "management, expenses, and risks of business". It seems that the latter, together with the author who translates *Zeyoona* as "losses", convey the most accurate descriptions of the term.

[9] *Kethuboth*, ibid., 66b.

[10] Consult, Adin Steinsaltz, *Iyunim, Kethuboth*, Vol. II:66b, where he comments on the talmudic expression "Zutar Zeyoona". Steinsaltz writes: " . . . some translate this expression as *Loss*. For in case of a big investment there are also bound to be big losses. And perhaps in cases such as these, there are big risks . . . (Rabbi J. Ben Minash)." (This quotation is a translation by the authors).

risk-taking husband the right to deny what is due because of his failure as an entrepreneur.

Risk-taking as a category of economic activity is not entirely absent in early Jewish literature outside the Talmud. For example, it is present in the Wisdom tradition as evidenced by the *Book of Ecclesiastes* (Qoheleth) 11:1–6. Again, it is treated in the Parable of the Talents (Matthew, 25:14–30). However, it emerges with particular clarity in talmudic concept of *Zeyoona*. In the treatment of the possibility of loss on investment of a wife's dowry, the husband is clearly categorised as the risk taker. *Zeyoona* is applicable strictly to the activities of the entrepreneur, and since the wife is not party to the entrepreneurship, her *Kethubah* premium is not in question. She is not the one who invests the capital.

What the wife's dowry offers the husband, if that dowry is in suitably liquid form, is the opportunity for risk-taking in business ventures. Her "reward" for creating that opportunity is the fifty percent premium. His "reward", if any, is a return on the assumption of business risk in the modern sense, i.e., a gamble on the possibility of gain or loss in an investment. Profit and loss are just two sides of the same coin, in that both stem from the risks that have been assumed by the entrepreneur. Such a firm appreciation of the role and incidence of risk in economic activity is rare in ancient literature.

The Concept of Uncertainty

Frank H. Knight (1885–1972) was the first major, modern economist to call attention to the distinction between "risk" and "uncertainty".[11] The former, he contended, is a "measurable uncertainty", whereas the latter is an "unmeasurable uncertainty". Uncertainty arises then, whenever a decision can lead to more than one possible consequence. The term "uncertainty" ought to be reserved for describing situations in which a reasonable estimate of the probability that some event will occur cannot be made. No one possesses knowledge of the future, so there are circumstances in which a decision-maker is either unwilling or unable to assign probability distributions of outcomes to various contemplated alternative actions. For example, if a person is seriously ill and the medical authorities are unwilling to make a reasonable estimate of the probability of that person's recovering, then the situation is uncertain (rather than risky) in medical terms. In such circum-

---

[11] F.H. Knight ibid.

stances, the decision maker must often rely on intuition and judgement.

Since Knight's pioneering investigations, economists have been in the forefront of endeavours to develop more precise explanations of the ways in which uncertainty affects human behaviour. Analysis has become more systematic and sophisticated.[12] However, in this respect it is notable that a recent, authoritative survey of this field of research concludes with the observation that, "Uncertainty *per se* really introduces little that is fundamentally new into economics . . ."[13] Perhaps this is the case, and the old Wisdom adage— "there is nothing new under the sun" (*Ecclesiastes* I:9)—holds in this instance. Certainly, as we shall show, the talmudic scholars had a strong grasp of the role of uncertainty in economic matters. Once again, the major focus of attention is debate concerning the *Kethubah* deed.

Uncertainty and the Kethubah

One of the major aspects of the marriage contract envisaged in the Talmud is that the husband is entitled to enjoy the fruits, natural or monetary, from certain properties which legally belong to his wife's estate. This provision applies as long as she is alive. Another aspect, it should be recalled, is that the *Kethubah* deed involves a monetary obligation which has to be restored to the wife, either upon the dissolution of the marriage or the death of the husband. This debt obligation is of particular significance since, for all practical intents and purposes, it is in some respects akin to a marketable security.

Indeed, the *Kethubah* may be likened to a bond. A bond will mature, and so does the *Kethubah*. A bond may be redeemed before maturity, so too, the *Kethubah*. Like a bond, the *Kethubah* has two prices: a par value and a market value. Like a bond, the price of the *Kethubah* is subject to fluctuation, depending on a number of variables of which some are measurable and some are subjective or psychological. Like a security, the deed can be an object of speculation with attendant potentials for gains or losses.

---

[12] A recent discussion is, Ronald A. Heiner, "Uncertainty, Behaviour and Economic Theory", *American Economic Review* (May 1985), pp. 391–402. See also, the accompanying commentary by K.D. Wilde, A.D. Le Baron and D. Israelsen, ibid., pp. 403–8.

[13] Peter J. Hammond, "Uncertainty", in J. Eatwell et al (eds.), *The New Palgrave: a Dictionary of Economics*, Vol. 4 (New York: Macmillan, 1987), pp. 728–33.

With these features of the contract in mind, we can begin to examine the Mishnaic passage which deals with the question of the valuation of the *Kethubah*. The circumstance addressed by the passage is one in which false witnesses are intending to cause financial damage to the husband. In aid of more lucid presentation, we employ the interpretive translation of the original text by Michael Rodkinson.[14] Further, in the analysis which follows we make full use of Rashi's extensive treatment of the passage under consideration.[15]

The passage is, as follows: "*Mishna* II: We testify that so and so has divorced his wife and has not paid the amount mentioned in the marriage contract (and that testimony is false). Although they have not done any damage, as the husband has to pay the marriage contract at some time, they are nevertheless not free from the following payment—namely, it is appraised how much one would risk for her marriage contract in case she would remain a widow or divorced. However, if she died while her husband is still alive, he would inherit her (and such an amount they have to pay)."[16]

The financial damage intended to the husband by the false witnesses was three-fold: (a) to make the husband pay the *Kethubah*; (b) to deprive him of the benefits he can enjoy from his wife's estate during her lifetime; and, (c) to deprive him of the inheritance in case she dies. Given biblical injunction (Deuteronomy 19:19), the false witnesses are now to be penalized to the extent of a sum equivalent to the amount of the intended damage. The question arises, then, as to how the penalty is to be appraised.

A general method of appraisement is suggested in the *Mishna*, but it is not specific as to *the way* in which the valuation is to be made. The issue is taken up in the *Gemara*, as follows:

> How should the appraisement be made? According to R. Hisda, the appraisement must be of the husband's (claims). And according to R. Nathan b. Oshia, of the wife's estate. Said R. Papa: It prevails that the appraisement should be as of the wife's, and only to the amount mentioned in her marriage contract, without, however, touching the

---

[14] M.L. Rodkinson (ed., and trans.), *New Edition of the Babylonian Talmud* (Boston: The Talmud Society, 1918), Vol. ix, *Tract Maccoth*, p. 4.
[15] The *halakhic* implications of this passage are explored in an interesting paper by Yehoshua Liebermann, "The Economics of *Kethubah* Valuation", *History of Political Economy*, 14, 4 (1983), pp. 519–528. The author considers the interpretations of a number of commentators including Rif, Maimonides, and Rashbam. However, the contribution of Rashi, which is of special interest to the historian of economic thought, is noted only in passing (p. 527, f.n. 18).
[16] M.L. Rodkinson, ibid. The original text of this *Mishna* is in *Makoth* 3a.

benefit which the husband has in the fruit of her estate while she is yet alive. (trans. M.L. Rodkinson).[17]

Despite the ambiguity surrounding the appraisement technique in the foregoing debate, one point which emerges with clarity is that the intended damage is to be evaluated in accordance with the *Kethuba-security's* current market value. However, this leaves open the further question of from whose perspective the value of the security is to be estimated. Is it to be from the perspective of the husband, or of the wife?

At this point, the factor of uncertainty enters the picture, since the alternate perspectives involve (literally) matters of life and death. As Rodkinson observes, "one can risk to buy the inheritance of a woman from her husband who would inherit her in case of her death when he is still alive; and one can also risk to buy this from the woman in case her husband dies first."[18] The purchaser of the *Kethubah* stands to lose his entire investment if the wife pre-deceases her husband, and the husband inherits her. Alternately, given that the *Kethubah* has been bought at some rate of discount, the purchaser may make a considerable gain by collecting the full value of the *Kethubah* in the event of the husband pre-deceasing or divorcing his wife.

The potential purchaser must also reckon with other contingencies. For example, he must take into account that there are substantial differences in the amounts that he is prepared to risk. It emerges, as we will see, that he would be prepared to pay more when buying from the husband than from the wife. In this regard, the element of probability asserts itself.

Uncertainty and the "Benefit of the Pleasure"

The distinguished eleventh century commentator, Rashi, considers the element of uncertainty in *Kethubah* valuation at length. There are two parts to his argument. The first places the emphasis on the role which uncertainty plays in the scheme of evaluation. The second combines uncertainty with the principle of *Tovath Hanoah* ("benefit of the pleasure").[19]

In regard to the scheme of evaluation, Rashi observes that both husband and wife have respective vested rights in the *Kethubah*.

---

[17] ibid.
[18] ibid.
[19] Consult, *Aruch Completum*, Vol. IV, p. 2. See also *Baba Kama*, 89a, and Rashi on the same.

However, each of those rights is beclouded by the condition of uncertainty. The situation is characterized by the facts that, as remarked above, "the wife figures that if the husband should die, she will collect the entire *Kethubah*, while the husband figures that if his wife should die, he will inherit her."[20] The circumstances are marked by a strong element of unpredictability.

Rashi goes on to assert that if the *Kethubah* is to be traded under such conditions of uncertainty, the husband's "uncertain claim" (*Z'Khut Sfaiko*) will command a higher price than the wife's "uncertain claim" (*Z'Khut Sfaikah*). There are two reasons which tell in favour of the husband's claim. First, as the "obligor"—as Rashi puts it —the husband is a *Mukhsak V'omed*: he is in "firm control" of the situation. Second, as long as the husband lives, he (and not his wife) can enjoy the usufruct from any field which he may have mortgaged to his wife as part of her *Kethubah*. Hence, when the husband wishes to sell his "uncertain claim", the discount from the face value of the *Kethubah* is likely to be minimal. On the other hand, when the wife wishes to sell her "uncertain claim", the discount is likely to be much steeper, if only for the fact that her status is that of a "potential claimant", which compounds the uncertainty.

The second part of Rashi's argument introduces the concept of the "benefit of the pleasure". In Rashi's view, the debaters in the *Gemara* who considered the case of the false witnesses (see above) were not concerned with the value of the entire *Kethubah* in question. Rather, they were concerned with the value of the "benefit of the pleasure" flowing from that *Kethubah*. The relevant question is: are the false witnesses to be penalized in terms of the wife's "benefit of the pleasure" or of the husband's "benefit of the pleasure"? Here, Rashi integrates the notion of "uncertain claims" with that of the "benefit of the pleasure". The latter concept requires some elucidation.

Ordinarily, the term *Tovath Hanoah* ("benefit of the pleasure") refers to a feeling of satisfaction which one derives from obliging somebody. For example, if one bestows a material favour on another person, the gratitude that this evokes on the part of the recipient, will have a pleasing effect on the benefactor.[21] However,

---

[20] See, Rashi, *Makhoth*, 3b., loc. cit.

[21] Whether or not the benefit of putting another person under obligation can be a monetary consideration is a subject of talmudic controversy. For an extensive review of the topic "Tovath Hanoah", see *Enziklopedia Talmudit* (in Hebrew), (Jerusalem, 1989), Vol. ix, pp. 99–144. Although apparently a comprehensive

within the context of the two states of "uncertainties " surrounding evaluation of the *Kethubah*, the term has a distinct meaning. *Tovath Hanoah* connotes the *difference* inherent in the two values of uncertainty, i.e., the differential in the value between *his* "uncertain claim" and/or in the value of *her* "uncertain claim".

The "benefit of the pleasure" is what one gains from selling the claim. This gain will be different as between husband and wife because of the difference in the uncertainties associated with their respective claims. As the gain is different, so there is a difference between the face value of the claim on maturity net of what the purchaser has paid, depending on whether the purchase has been from the husband or from the wife.

There are definitions of *Tovath Hanoah* in the latter context in both the Babylonian Talmud (notably in *Baba-Kama*, 89a) and the *Tosephta*.[22] However, the clearest definition is provided in the Jerusalem Talmud, namely: "how much will a purchaser be willing to risk for the Kethubah (under conditions of uncertainty) contingent on the probability that either the wife might die while he is alive, or that the husband might die and the purchaser will realize the full amount of the Kethubah."[23] What distinguishes Rashi's interpretation, in the light of this and the other definitions, is his explicit integration of *Tovath Hanoah* and the idea of "uncertain claims". Further, in so doing, he facilitated the development of a framework within which those "uncertainties" could be calculated.

Computing Uncertain Values

In the 1920's, Frank H. Knight wrote that in a state of uncertainty, probabilities are not known and cannot be predicted, so in business-life the uncertain returns from an investment may be known but the probabilities of distribution will be unknown.[24] Yet, some nine hundred years before this, the integration achieved by Rashi provided an instrument whereby there could be attempts at computation in objective terms of the present values of the economic uncertainties associated with the *Kethubah* contract. These

---

treatment of this subject, it is surprising that the editors have virtually omitted the presentation of "Tovath Hanoah" in the context of the Kethubah evaluation and the different meaning that is attached to it there.

[22] See, *Tosephta*, Makhoth, Ch. 1:4. The *Tosephta* (Aram. "Editions") is a Tannaitic work which often provides variant reading of the Mishna.

[23] T. Jerusalem, Makhot, lb. The quotation has been freely translated by the authors.

[24] F.H. Knight, op. cit., pp. 232–4.

attempts were mainly, but not exclusively, a province of the contributors to *Tosaphot*. The tosaphists flourished from the twelfth to the
fourteenth century.[25]

Tosaphot adopted Rashi's thesis that the husband, in his role of
"obligor", can be presumed to be in "firm control", whereas his
wife is only a potential claimant.[26] Consequently, the husband's
"uncertain claim" will command a much higher market price than
the wife's "uncertain claim". On this basis, and assuming that the
par value of the *Kethubah* is 1,000 *denarii*, the tosaphists found that if
the husband wishes to sell his claim (which claim turns on the
possibility of his wife's dying and his inheriting her) the asset will
be traded at a fifty percent discount, i.e., for five hundred *denarii*.
On the other hand, if the wife, who is in the weaker position, wishes
to sell her claim (turning on the possibility of the death of her
husband or on his divorcing her) it will sell at a sixty percent
discount, i.e., for four hundred *denarii*. The *Tosaphot* adds that if the
wife should sell her claim to her husband (or to someone else) at a
discount rate of sixty percent, the holder of the asset will realize
1,000 denarii (400 plus 600) at its maturity.

The foregoing numerical extensions also serve to clarify Rashi's
interpretation of the debate in the *Gemara* concerning the financial
penalties to be imposed on the false witnesses (see above). On the
calculations of the tosaphists, the wife's "benefit of the pleasure"
will be 400 *denarii*, leaving a remainder of 600 *denarii* as compared
with the par value of the *Kethubah*. However, the husband's "benefit
of the pleasure" will be 500 denarii, leaving a remainder of 500. Are
the false witnesses liable for 600 or 500 *denarii* by way of damages?
This depends on whether the wife's or the husband's perspective is
adopted as the base for assessment.

Expectation in Contemporary Economics

In an imperfect world, expectations play an important role in all
areas of human endeavour. What individuals or firms believe is
going to happen in the future will necessarily affect the choices they
make in the present. Whenever one travels, one expects to return

---

[25] *Tosaphot* (Heb. "additions") are the *Novellae* on the Talmud and are printed
in the outer column of all Talmud editions.

[26] The husband's "control", it can be added, is partly a function of the law
regarding divorce. As Y. Liebermann observes (op. cit., p. 524): " . . . according
to ancient Jewish law the husband is given the power to control divorce decisions.
Clearly, this means that the husband has more information than any other party
as to whether and as to when he intends to divorce his wife."

safely. When individuals or firms make investment decisions, they expect a profit. When governments try to control the vagaries of the business cycle, their efforts are accompanied by an aura of expectation. All these decisions are rooted in beliefs, views or guesses—educated or uneducated—out of which the matrix of expectations is formed.

Reflections on the formation and consequences of expectations are common to all forms of literature, ancient and modern. Yet, during the 1970's some economists forged an approach to expectational phenomena which represents an extension of neo-classical economic treatment. This approach is generally known as "the theory of rational expectation".[27]

Before the 1970's, the dominant hypothesis amongst economists was that of "adaptive expectation" (or error learning). The employment of this hypothesis extends back (although not in name) to Irving Fisher (1911), and its basic tenet is that people rely upon the past to predict the future. Hence, the actual happenings of the two or three years in the immediate past with respect to variables such as prices and climate will determine the expectations of people concerning the future state of those variables. It is also allowed that if forecast errors have been made in the past, e.g., individuals, firms or unions have underestimated the rate of inflation to pertain, then expectations will be adjusted accordingly.

By contrast, the rational expectation hypothesis does not limit the formation of expectations to reflections on past events. It proposes that people not only learn from their mistakes but also alter their behaviour as additional information becomes available. People engage in rational forecasting of what is going to happen in the future. They use the available information to *manage their anticipation*. In the case of a stimulus—be that stimulus policy—generated or otherwise—people will safeguard their own interests by neutralizing the effect of the stimulus where necessary.[28]

---

[27] The extensive economic literature which appeared during the 1970's is reviewed in, Brian Kantor, "Rational Expectation and Economic Thought", *Journal of Economic Literature*, Vol. XVII (December 1979), pp. 1422–41.

[28] Among the leading contributors to the development of the rational expectation theory are Robert Lucas (Chicago), and Thomas Sargent and Neil Wallace (Minnesota). A prominent economist associated with the adaptive expectations theory is Milton Friedman. On the theory of expectations in Economics, consult, J. Eatwell et al. (eds) op. cit., Vol. 2, pp. 20, 79–85, and 224–9. See also, Kenneth E. Boulding, *Economic Analysis: Microeconomics*, Vol. I (New York: Harper and Row, 1966), pp. 691–5.

Rational Expectation in the Talmud

One of the basic elements of the theory of rational expectation is
that in decision making on economic matters, an individual will
make use of all the available and relevant information for the
purpose of forming a view about the future. This aspect of the
theory is also given prominence in the discussion of economic issues
in the Talmud. Further, the Talmud displays an appreciation of
the role which the systematic gathering of information can play in
enhancing one's control over one's economic future.

An illustration of the latter appreciation is afforded by the strand
of talmudic thought in which an agricultural cycle theory began to
take shape (see Chapter 4, sect: "Cycles, Stars and Harvests").
There R. Johanan urged engagement in calculations concerning
"cycles of the seasons and constellations". This recommendation,
according to later commentators, was given so that agricultural
cycles, and hence fluctuations of business conditions in general,
could be more accurately anticipated. These were phenomena that
could be rationally expected, and which could be more readily dealt
with by those who were in command of forecast data.

Emphasis on the need to take account of all available information to ensure one's economic future is illustrated by some of the
contributors to the discussion of *Kethubah*. For example, R. Isaac
Alfasi (1013–1103) quotes R. Hai Gaon's comments on the *Gemara*
debate, as follows:

" . . . This appears to be the case: R. Hisda maintains that the
appraisement is made on the basis of the husband's claims means,
is he old which by the state of nature he is more likely to die than
young men; is he ill or in good health; is he well to do so that he
might be inclined to divorce his wife and pay her Kethubah; do
they quarrel or not . . . and R. Nathan b. Oshia, who asserts 'on
the woman's estate', maintains the very opposite; is *she* ill or well; is
she old or young . . . for when one bargains for this kind of object,
one will estimate it on the basis of those variables. And R. Papa
added to R. Nathan's argument—is her estate large, so that the
buyer of her Kethubah who bets on her future marital status (that
she will be widowed or divorced), will be inclined to risk more of his
financial capital, or does she have little where the risk is
minimal . . ."[29]

In this passage, Alfasi goes beyond the notion of the measurabil-

---

[29] Consult, *Alfasi Digest*, along with the commentary of RAN (Rabbenu Nissim-
Geronde, 12th century). The translation of the above passage is by the authors.

ity of the "benefit of the pleasure" (see above) in order to predict an uncertain future. Quantification alone, he suggests, is an insufficient tool in such a complicated realm of decision-making. The careful investor also seeks out beforehand all the available information which is relevant to the outcome of the given transaction. The investor must be concerned not merely with the prediction of future occurrences but also with the way the forecast is made.

Generally then, the prospective purchaser of a *Kethubah*, before embarking upon a course of action, and as each case may require, should gather all available information pertaining to such factors as the husband's or wife's physical, social and psychological status, including age, health, material well being, and temper. Armed with this comprehensive information the decision-maker will be able to make a more rational forecast about the future outcome of the investment.

Review

This chapter has been concerned, in the main, with the economic implications of the talmudic analysis of the problem of *Kethubah* evaluation. In the first place, we showed that the talmudic Rabbis displayed profound insight and very considerable sophistication regarding the manifestation of the "risk" factor called *Zeyoona*. This concept is closely interrelated with the business phenomena of "profit" and "loss". These two are just alternate sides of the same coin, in that both stem from the risks that have been assumed by the entrepreneur.

Secondly, in the rabbinic treatment of "uncertainty", the contribution of Rashi, in particular, was emphasized. That contribution displays a discernible modernity in its approach to the computation of uncertainties. By employing the concept of the "benefit of the pleasure", Rashi opened the way to reasoning in categories of measurable uncertainty that are quantifiable and objective, as against an unmeasurable uncertainty, which is intuitive and subjective. Finally, we remarked on points of contact between rational expectation theory and certain talmudic emphases in dealing with economic behaviour. Those points comprised management of the future through rational forecasting, and awareness of the role of information in the formation of expectations.

PART FOUR

THE VALUES OF PERSONS

CHAPTER EIGHT
CATEGORIES OF VALUE

As the late Joan Robinson observed: "One of the greatest meta-physical ideas in economics is expressed in the word 'value'."[1] Hence, historians of economic thought have been obliged to pay special attention to the on-going metaphysical discourse surrounding that idea, from the ancient Greek philosophers through to the marginal utility theorists and beyond. Despite the continuing concern of those historians, however, the wide-ranging treatments of the problem of value in Talmudic literature have been given scant attention by them.

The dialectics of the Rabbinic scholars were meticulously coordinated by a complex system of value concepts, rooted in concrete human experience.[2] In this chapter, we wish to draw attention to the manner in which the Rabbis dealt with the subjective-objective dichotomy in the concept of value. Also, we show how they came to formulate a unique value category which can be termed *price-less value*, or, even more paradoxically, *valueless value*.

Subjective and Objective Value

The Talmudic treatment of the dichotomy relating to value is bound up with the investigation of "human life value", as conceptualized in the terms *erekh nephashot*.[3] This investigation had a biblical base in the practice of "consecration of the value of human life to the Lord" (see, *Leviticus* 27: 1–8). The practice, it can be observed, brings together three distinct entities: value; human life; and, Deity. The first of these entities is subjective, the second combines both the subjective and objective, whilst the third is objective.

The biblical term for value is *erekh*, and since value is a category of human experience that motivates action, it must necessarily be

---

[1] J. Robinson, *Economic Philosophy* (1964), p. 26.
[2] See, M. Kadushin, *The Rabbinic Mind* (New York: Jewish Theological Seminary of America, 1952), pp. 97 ff. Consult also, A. Lelyveld, "A Distinctive Value", *Journal of Reform Judaism* (Fall, 1978), pp. 3 ff.
[3] Literally, this means the "value" or "valuation of human life". This theme is taken up, at length, in Chapter Nine.

subjective. However, human life is a composite of a subjective-objective phenomenon. The thought underlying this latter is best appreciated by reflection on the anthropological meaning of the early biblical term *nephesh*, which noun appears in the Bible on 754 occasions.[4] According to Daniel Lys's investigation, *nephesh*, "has several meanings: life, what lives and dies, desire and pleasure, the feeling . . . the breath: the animate living being and the self I."[5] Here, there is no Platonic dualism which views the "soul" as distinct from the "body". Rather, the biblical *nephesh* embraces the totality of life, body and soul, vitality and potentiality.[6] Human life is thus a composite embracing both the subjective and the objective. The third entity is the Deity which, for the biblical writers and the talmudists alike, represents the absolute, the abstract, the spiritual, a distinct objective experience.

In their reflections on the practice which brought together these three diverse categories, the Rabbis found it necessary to introduce a fourth. There was a need to find a common denominator, and to concretise the valuation process. For these purposes the yardstick of money was employed. This introduction of money, however, gave rise to a further problem. The Talmudic doctors, who functioned within a religious universe of discourse, were confronted with a major question: how to reconcile the spiritual with the mundane—how to reconcile the celestial purpose of human valuation with the terrestrial practice of monetary quantification.

As they worked toward a reconciliation, the talmudists sometimes expressed sharply opposing views, without compromising the spirit of the texts with which they were engaged. One school of thought emphasized the spiritual dimensions of the problem. The other school was more impressed by the mundane, and hence, the economic aspects of the debate in hand. Together, these schools achieved a balance between the abstract and the concrete, between objectivity and subjectivity. Neither fully embraced one or other of the extreme poles of the subject-object matrix. Rather, together they objectivised the subjective elements and subjectivised the

---

[4] In the Septuagint, the earliest Greek version of the Bible (composed c. 270 BC), the noun *nephesh* is translated on about 680 occasions as "psyche". This latter is more akin to the Hebrew term *ruakh*, or, spirit.

[5] Consult, D. Lys, "The Israelite Soul According to the LXX", *Vetus Testamentum*, Vol. XVI, No. 1 (January 1965), pp. 183–228.

[6] It is noteworthy that in *Leviticus* the term *nephesh* is also used in reference to a "dead body". On the other hand, the same term is also used as a synonym for "soul". Further, Saadia Gaon (882–942), for example, employs this term in a purely metaphysical sense. He writes, "Who verifies to man with certainty the existence of their soul (naphshotom). *Emunot V'deot*, p. 4.

objective. The manner in which they achieved a symbiosis is explored in the sections which follow.

Objectifying The Subjective Strand

Over the course of the rabbinic debate, some of the sages tended to
spiritualize the *entire* conception of the scriptural valuation. In
other words, they found it possible to treat not only the Deity, but
also value, human life, and even money in objective terms. They
emphasized one side of the value spectrum through objectifying the
subjective.

Scriptural valuation was spiritualized partly by means of the
attribution of a special quality to the word *erekh*. The term was
taken to stand for the expression of an *ideal* value. Although this
value may be derived basically from the economic utility of the
person, nonetheless it is also independent of economic considerations. Hence, men, women, slaves and children, depending on their
age, are thought to have a *fixed* value. Such value is objective in
character and discrete in application.

To reinforce this thesis, the Talmudic writers used an anlytical
refinement to support the definition of the biblical *erekh* in objective
terms. With *Leviticus* 27: 1–8 as a point of departure, the *Mishna-
Arakhin* commences with the following clause:

"ALL (persons) "ma-arikhin'—are fit to evaluate 'v'ne-
arakhin'—or are to be made subject of evaluation, 'nodrin'—are fit
to vow (another's worth), 'v' nidrin'—or have their worth vowed."[7]

Here, the Talmud is distinguishing between two terms—*erekh*
and *neder*, i.e., between valuation and vow. The former is said to be
a sacred mode of expression. However, the latter is considered a
secular designation, and hence is subject to the operation of the
market forces relevant to the person vowed.[8] In other words, the
expression *neder* is synonymous with a "monetary" vow (d'mai).
Consequently, the subject vowed is to be evaluated in *subjective*
terms, i.e., in terms of what the market will fetch. By contrast, *erekh*
is deemed to be "a consecration" where the valuation terms are
fixed and, therefore, is categorized as an ideal, or objective, value.

The latter valuation, it is clear, is considered to be super-

---

[7] This quote, and subsequent quotations, are taken largely from the Babylonian
Talmud Arakhin, Soncino Press, tr. Leo Yung, with minor renditions by the present
authors.

[8] See, Rashi, *Arakhin*, 2a, *op. cit.*, also, *Tossaphot, ibid.* (*Tossaphot* is a composite
commentary by the disciples of Rashi (d. 1105), supplementing that of their
master).

mundane. Hence, it is independent of the person's physical or mental condition. To underline this last point, the Talmud deduces that even an utterly disfigured person, whose market value is zero, is still subject to scriptural valuation norms.[9] In general then, *erekh* has been objectified by means of Talmudic deduction, and this despite the fact that *erekh* is an act of valuation which is clearly derived from the economic utility of the subject.

Objectification of Nephesh

Spiritualization of the conception of scriptural valuation did not turn merely on the objectification of *erekh*. It also involved objectification of the term *nephesh*, which, as was remarked above, is an early scriptural noun describing a combination of subjective and objective attributes inherent within a person. Moreover, in later Talmudic and Aggadic literature, the same term was sometimes applied to a dead person.

Given these usages of the term, both early and late, it might be supposed that *nephesh* could not be objectified. How could the spiritual component be singled out for special treatment? That component must be kept part of, and yet apart from, the physical component, if it is to be evaluated independently and in monetary terms. Yet, the sages achieved an objectification by distinguishing between the person *per se* and his or her personality. It is the personality that is subject to valuation, not the person.

The talmudic scholars attained the foregoing distinction partly by strongly emphasizing the existence of a divine spark in man. Further, they boldly replaced the relative term *nephesh* with the absolute term *neshamah*, i.e. with "soul" in a metaphysical sense.[10] They substituted the transcendental for the transient. There are very many examples of this substitution, and one such is located in

---

[9] This deduction involves some significant issues which are considered in the concluding section of this chapter.

[10] See, Talmud, Ber. 10a, where *neshama* is subtly but deliberately substituted for *nephesh*. The Talmud and the Midrash frequently compared the relation of the soul to the body to the relation of God to the world. For example, "As God is pure so also the soul is pure. As God dwells in the inmost part of the universe, so also the soul dwells in the inmost part of the body." Although in both Talmudin the term *neshamah* is sometimes used simply to indicate human or even animal life (T. Yerusl. B. Kama, VII, end, 6a), its predominant usage is in a spiritual sense. Most symptomatic is Rabbi Simai's statement (c. 200 CE), " . . . of all earthly creatures their bodies and souls are earthly except man's, for his body is earthly, but his soul is divine." (Sifrei, Deut., Hazinu, parg. 306, f., 132a). There are many more references in Midrashic, and especially in cabalistic literature, which view *neshamah* in transcendental terms.

Arakhin 4b. Here, the question is raised: what if one dedicates (to the Lord) just the head of a person, how much is to be paid? The consensus reply is: the worth of the entire person, because the *neshamah* is attached to it (*"Davar she-ha-neshama t'luya bo"*). The subtle change of terms here is notable. The abstract *neshamah* now takes the place of the anthropological *nephesh*, since, as the Talmud states, man must be valued in accordance with his "highest dignity" (*B'khvodo*, where Rashi explains it as *L'fee khvodo*).[11]

Objectification of Money

Having objectified both value and human life, the rabbis still faced the problem of objectifying money. The currency unit of the time was the shekel, and since this was a silver coin, its metallic content might be thought to give the unit an intrinsic value which renders it objective. However, such an understanding would be obliged to ignore fluctuations in the price of silver rendering the unit subjective, i.e., influenced by market mechanisms. To solve this problem the talmudists deduced analogically that the valuation process with which they were concerned was to be consummated in "holy currency" (*b'shekel ha-kodesh*). By this device, the objectivist school of talmudic thought was able to reduce the problem of the fluctuations in the price of silver to an accidental aspect of the problem which they were addressing. They maintained their position by focussing on the nominal character of a given standard of value.

The device of the objectivist school involved the establishment of a value category which is institutional in form and discrete in application. Much the same device, it can be remarked, was employed by the early Schoolmen, including Thomas Aquinas, in their approach to the question of usury.[12] Further, it can be remarked that the objectified version of biblical evaluation was adopted subsequently in varying degrees by many exegetes and commentators in the talmudic tradition up to modern times. Among the more modern commentators to espouse the objective approach in a doctrinaire fashion was the German-Jewish biblical commentator, Samson R. Hirsch (1808–1888). For Hirsch, *Torah* is an objective reality, and given this understanding he writes:

---

[11] In approximately the same period when the Talmud was compiled, St. Augustine also ascribes to man a "nature of the highest dignity", which appellation is used frequently in the Talmud. See, Augustine's *The City of God*, Book XI: 16. This work was written between 413–426 C.E.

[12] On this, see, B. Gordon, *Economic Analysis Before Adam Smith* (London: Macmillan, 1975), pp. 163–165.

"*Erekh*, and especially *Erkheha* is an expression of an ideal, imaginary value . . . a person has to God and his Sanctuary. This value is given as a fixed one. It has absolutely nothing to do with physical, spiritual, intellectual, moral or social qualities. It rises and falls purely according to sex and age. This universal equality is already expressed in the term—*erkheha nephashot*. It is only *nephashot* as such which are to be considered, and every living person is a *nephesh*."[13]

This statement by Hirsch presents one of the ancient approaches to the problem of valuation. However, as a position on that problem it is suspect on etymological grounds. In particular, his assertion that, "every living person is a *nephesh*" is not accord with the application of *nephesh* to a dead body by the ancients. For example, in *Leviticus* 21:1, the word *nephesh* means "a dead body". Again, *Leviticus* 21:11 states explicitly, "v'al kol naphshot met . . .", which precisely means "a dead body". The identical understanding is expressed in the Talmudic tractate, *Nazir* 49 a-b.

Subjectifying the Objective Strand

As the stance of Samson Hirsch illustrates, the objective approach to the establishment of value has continued on well into the modern era of talmudic commentary. Nevertheless, there is a tradition which supports an alternate, subjective approach. This tradition surfaces most clearly in the writings of the outstanding R. Judah Loew b. Bezalel, who was known as the Maharal of Prague (c. 1525–1609). However, the Maharal's contributions look back to those of some earlier scholars.

Among the ancients, the third-century Palestinian, Hezekiah might be cited as an anticipator since he emphasized the different working capacities of men and women in conjunction with the question of dedication of human life value. For example, he referred to the propensity of women as compared with men, for health and longevity. Hezekiah was by no means oblivious to the spiritual aspect of the practice of dedication, but he also seemed to have been aware that this act of religious proclivity is intimately related to the issue of economic utility. He seems to have retained in his thought the original meaning of *nephesh*, a meaning which referred to a person whose worth was contingent on his or her working powers within the framework of a specific life cycle.[14]

---

[13] S.R. Hirsch, *The Pentateuch*, Vol. III, *Leviticus* (Part II), translated by Isaac Levy, (London, 1958), p. 812.

[14] *Arakhin*, 19a.

In Talmud *Arakhin*, 19a, the following question is asked: why is it that when a man reaches the age 60, his value diminishes by *more* than one-third (i.e., from 50 to 15 shekels), whereas the value of a female declines only to one-third (i.e., from 30 to 10 shekels)? Responding to this question, Hezekiah offers an economic answer: "People say, an old man in the house is a liability in the house, while an old woman in the house is an asset in the house." The inference from Hezekiah's statement is clear. At various stages of the life cycle, people are endowed with various working and/or earning capacities, hence the highest ratings are for persons in their prime (20–60). However, women, in contrast to men at the age of sixty and beyond, generally enjoy better health and are therefore able to perform useful work for a longer period of time. It follows from this that in the case of women, the rate of depreciation is less.

Another anticipator of the Maharal's analysis was the eleventh-century master, Rashi. Commenting on the relevant passages of *Leviticus* concerning dedication, he explains the valuation in spiritual terms when he addresses the third verse of the biblical text. However, this is not the case when he considers the seventh verse. Here, he interprets the life-cycle in Hezekiah's utilitarian terms. Rashi, it would appear, intended that both the spiritual and the utilitarian must be equally represented. There is both an abstract, or objective, value, and a utilitarian or subjective, value present. He implies that there is a functional relationship between the two. Rashi sought to integrate objective and subjective value elements, and to demonstrate that precepts derived from ethics can be harmonized with economic practice.[15]

This dualistic approach was adopted later in the commentary on *Leviticus* by Abrabanel, which was published in Venice in 1579. Isaac b. Juda Abrabanel (1437–1508) was a Lisbon-born biblical exegete, philosopher, statesman and financier who was familiar with the writings of leading Christian theologians, and was influenced by the currents of humanism abroad in the Renaissance. His interpretations and investigations reflect the medieval spirit of scholasticism as well as the social structure of the European society of the day.

Abrabanel placed "the way of the Torah" side by side with "the scientific" and "the analytic". Hence, in his treatment of dedication in *Leviticus*, he gives first priority to the spiritual version of the biblical valuation schema, although his argument is couched in

---

[15] See, Rashi, loc. cit., 19a. This issue is also discussed in the commentary on the Torah by Elijah Mizrachi (d. 1540).

humanistic terms. However, he then proceeds to interpret "valuation" from a biological point of view. Not only does he point to physical and mental differences between men and women, but, most remarkably, he puts special emphasis on the female's reproductive capacity. Abrabanel writes:

"Actually, the highest physical and mental vigour of a male is between 20–60. His worth is therefore estimated 50 shekels. Inasmuch as it takes two women to do the heavy work of a single strong, muscular man, a female should have an estimated value half that of a male, i.e., 25 shekels. However, since a female in her primary years has the capacity to conceive and to give birth, the Torah has given her a premium of 5 shekels. Thus, her estimated total worth is 30 shekels."[16]

This emphasis on the reproductive capacity of a woman, and the *agio* which Abrabanel was prepared to attribute to it, may reflect prevailing mercantilist ideas regarding the importance of an expanding population to ensure economic growth. A women who gives birth can be regarded as a productive agent whose productivity warrants a return.

The same writer goes on to discuss the various attributes and shortcomings of both males and females, given various phases of their life-cycles. In this, he is following in the foot-steps of both Hezekiah and Rashi. There is the same concern to integrate the logical and the theological. However, Abrabanel may be accounted innovative, not only in what he said but how he said it. Certainly, he was orthodox in belief, but he was heterodox by way of method.

An even more striking innovation on the question of valuation was undertaken by the Maharal of Prague. Writing in the sixteenth century, this lone but prolific scholar developed his own philosophy as well as a new method of presentation. A radically new approach to the *Leviticus* verses flowed from these.

Unlike all the interpreters who preceded him, the Maharal ventured to explain Scripture's valuation in psychological terms. In so doing he put forward an explicitly subjective theory of value. This was achieved by placing emphasis on the subjective valuation of the priest, which valuation figures prominently in the biblical text, Maharal's position is summarized in the following:

"Scripture's repeated emphasis on the pronoun '*thy* valuation' strongly suggests a value judgement which is necessarily relative and subjective. The process of valuation of persons according to

---

[16] Abrabanel, *Commentary on Leviticus XXVII* (Jerusalem, 1924), p. 176. This extract is freely translated by the authors.

their age and sex does not at all contradict this view, for it simply implies 'a judgemental valuation of man's worth which in this case is fixed'. The fact that in the subsequent cases of dedication of fields, houses and other objects, the stress is repeatedly put on the pronoun 'thy valuation' and 'as the priest shall value it, so shall it stand' only confirms this thesis that valuation in general is contingent on the "psychological" factor which is inherently subjective."[17]

The novelty of this approach is its emphasis on the crucial role which the "individual" plays in the valuation scheme. Accordingly, it is the principle of individual valuation which is the most important factor in the decision-making process. As Maharal states:

"In truth, any (economic) valuation is performed by individuals. Now, sometimes one person may estimate an object for so much, while another person may estimate the very same object for a different amount . . . Since valuation is subject to the feelings of individuals, it is inevitably subjective and 'psychological'."[18]

This understanding of the foundations of value, it can be remarked, has much in common with that of the marginal utility school which emerged in Economics in the latter part of the nineteenth century. Like Maharal, members of that school stressed the subjective and individualistic in the formation of value. For example, Friedrich von Wieser (1851–1926) wrote:

"To tell the truth , there is no 'objective' exchange value . . . The classical school gave no further attention to the 'subjective' value . . . only objective exchange value was considered worthy of scientific investigation . . . The individualistic school reduced everything in the social economy to individual effort . . . yet it failed to realise that economic action is a confluence of individual valuations."[19]

For both the Austrian, von Wieser and the fifteenth-century Talmudic scholar, value is rooted in the subjective. The estimation of value is essentially a matter of individual decision-making.

---

[17] Jodah Loew, or Maharal, *Gur Aryeh* ("Yehadut" edition, Israel, 1972), Vol. III, p. 196. The first edition was published as a commentary on Rashi in 1578. The quoted extract is translated by the authors from the Hebrew text with minor renditions. It should be noted that the term "psychological" is not used by the Maharal. Nevertheless, it is a term which best expresses the sense of his analysis.

[18] op. cit., cf. p. 196. The quoted extract is freely translated from the Hebrew original.

[19] F. von Wieser, *Social Economics*, translated by A. Ford Hinricks (New York: Kelley, 1967), p. 235.

The Doctrine of a Valueless Value

A particularly striking aspect of the talmudic debate on the consecration of human life is the emergence within it of the idea of a "valueless value". To appreciate the background for this idea it is necessary to recall the first clause of *Arakhin*, which was discussed above. There, the rabbis distinguished between *erekh*, "valuation", and *neder*, "vow", and hence, between an ideal value and a market value. In their reasoning, *erekh* is analogous to "objective value" in an ethical sense, whereas *neder* is akin to "subjective value" is an economic sense.

The first clause of *Arakin* states that ALL persons may be evaluated, and this statement is taken up for closer inspection. A questioner asks:

"What does ALL (Persons) are fit to be made subject to valuation mean to include? It is meant to include a person disfigured or one afflicted with boils. For one might have assumed that since Scripture says: "A vow . . . according to thy valuation', that only such persons that are fit to be made subject of a vow (as regards their worth) are fit to be made subjects of valuation, and persons that are unfit to be made subjects of a vow (as regards to their worth) are also unfit to be made subjects of valuation, hence Scripture informs us "of persons", i.e. no matter who they are."[20]

The principal issue here is the dichotomy represented by an economic variable, i.e., "vow", as against an ethical constant, i.e., "valuation". The passage points out that in view of the scriptural juxtaposition of these two contradictory terms, one might be led to the notion that ethical qualification depends on economic quantification. Since a "person disfigured or one affected with boils" has absolutely no "market" value, he or she is, therefore, unfit to be made subject of valuation (to the sanctuary). However, this is said to be erroneous. The adjective ALL is seen as forestalling such a mistaken inference by stipulating that even a person without a market price is endowed with certain attributes and, therefore, is subject of valuation.

---

[20] See, *Arakhin*, 2a and 4b; also Rosh Hashana 5b: Hulin 2a, upon which Rashi comments, "They (the disfigured . . .) are fit to vow (another's worth) but are not fit to have their own worth vowed since they are worthless". Similar explanations are given by Rashi in the Tractates. *Tossaphot* likewise explains it in the same vein, and Gershon b. Judah, surnamed Meor ha-Golah (ca. 965–1028), amplifies " . . . because no one wants to buy them." Many of the latter's explanations are embedded in Rashi's commentary on the Talmud. Compare Maimonides, *Hilkhot Arakhin V'khamamim*, chapter I, 8 and 9. Also his commentary on the *Mishna Arakhin*, chapter I, p. 5.

The ethical connotation of this analysis is explicit. In the realm of ultimate values there is to be no distinction between the physically fit and the "disfigured", between the healthy and the handicapped. Nor does such valuation distinguish between saint and sinner, learned and simple, or any such contrasting categories of persons, for their value is fixed according to their "highest dignity". Ultimate, or ideal, value should not be confused with market value.

Much the same differentiation between types of value may be found in the Scholastic tradition. For example, in his observations on Aristotle's *Ethics*, Thomas Aquinas states (Book V, Lect. 9) that the rank-order of values in nature and creation can be very different from the order derived from human calculations concerning the utility of goods. The latter order ranks a pearl ahead of a mouse, but a mouse is superior in terms of nature and creation. A similar comment on value occurs in the *Summa Theologica* by way of a reference to *The City of God* by Augustine of Hippo. Aquinas notes that a human slave is a superior being to a horse. However, in some circumstances, a horse may have a greater market value than that of a slave, since the horse is regarded as more useful.[21] Elsewhere, Aquinas distinguishes between "human goods" and "goods of soul" (*Summa*, 1–11, q. 4a, 7).[22] This too is a form of differentiation which correspond to that of the talmudic scholars.

While the parallels between the talmudic and scholastic traditions on value are evident, it may be claimed that in their debates, the talmudists took a step which was beyond those of any of the schoolmen. They endeavoured to forge a link between ethical value and economic value by applying a money sum to the former. The talmudists assigned a monetary value to the "disfigured" who, for all practical intents and purposes, did not possess any market value whatsoever. This meant that something which is economically valueless may still command economic value.

In this respect the Talmudic doctors opened up a route to thought on the economic status of the disadvantaged which the Schoolmen did not explore. The Schoolmen had ready to hand the long-standing imperatives concerning self-less Charity derived from the teachings of Jesus. Those imperatives could be invoked as offering the groundwork for a solution to the problems of the disadvantaged, despite the logic of market evaluation. Talmudic

---

[21] Thomas Aquinas, *Summa theologica*, II-II, qu. 77, art. 2, ad. 3. For Augustine, see, *The City of God*, XI, 16.

[22] For discussion, consult, S. T. Worland, *Scholasticism and Welfare Economics* (Notra Dame, 1967), pp. 27–34 ff.

scholars however, looked to a much more integral solution which combined both economic rationality and regard for those for whom the strict application of economic rationality would consign to the status of non-persons. The Talmudic scholars, it can be claimed, looked forward to the advent of Welfare Economics in its modern form.

In their deliberations on the consecration of human life, the talmudists endeavoured to account for both objective and subjective evaluation, and to bring these into meaningful relationship. They endeavoured to combine both the normative and the positive in arriving at a coherent response to what Scripture seemed to demand with respect to the custom involved. This attempt to bring together normative and positive is also characteristic of the modern economist who wishes to unite his or her research on subjectively-based economic behaviour with a regard for objective criteria. As S.T. Worland explains, welfare economics adds another dimension of evaluation to that of Economics in the conventional, modern sense. He writes:

"What distinguishes welfare economics from the rest of economic theory is its specific and characteristic concern, not with scientific explanation or description, but with normative appraisal or evaluation. Whereas pure theory tries merely to explain and predict, welfare economics intends to evaluate-to determine which economic phenomena, relationships, and practices deserve to be considered 'economically good' and desirable."[23]

It may also be contended that the Talmudic tradition, with its doctrine of a "valueless value", not only comprehends but also goes beyond the framework of Welfare Economics as it is understood today. Modern welfare theory is devoted to the question of how best to maximize social welfare. However, the theory is formulated in terms of considerations concerning positive economic value. Can such considerations encompass "valueless value"?

The problem here may be summarized, as follows. Economically, the valuation of totally incapacitated persons in terms of a positive sum actually amounts to a quantification of a negative value. Yet, the Talmudic novelty is vested in the notion that even such a value has psycho-economic characteristics. It might be argued that the value is analogous to that which underlies the modern idea of a negative income tax. However, whereas the latter line of thought is usually associated with policy stances that blend social concern with the provision of incentives to work, no such

---

[23] op. cit., p. 4.

stance is implied by the talmudists. Rather, they have established a distinct category in which the valueless subject is given a positive numerical value in economic terms. The category seems to have no counterpart in other pre-modern economic thought, nor in modern welfare economics.

CHAPTER NINE

HUMAN CAPITAL ISSUES

Since the 1960's, the concept of "human capital" has become an increasingly familiar idea for modern economists. Analysis related to this concept has had significant applications with respect to issues concerning the supply of labour and its remuneration. The applications have also gone further afield within contemporary thought.[1]

Historians of Economics have been quick to point out that despite the absence of reference to human capital considerations in neo-classical economics, some earlier economists were alive to the possibilities of this line of investigation.[2] Among the Mercantilists there was considerable emphasis on "art and ingenuity", i.e., the resource of skilled manpower, as a factor in national economic growth. Characteristically, Sir William Petty (1632–87) went so far as to attempt to develop measures of this resource.

In fact, reflection on the phenomenon of human capital formation and its implications extends back much further than the mercantilist era. There is little of relevance in this respect to be found in the writings of the Schoolmen of the middle ages and the renaissance, since the focus of the bulk of their economic analyses was the question of justice in exchange transactions between individuals. However, contemporary, and earlier, writers in the Jewish tradition were obliged to adopt a broader focus, and it is to these that the pioneering efforts concerning the economics of human capital must be ascribed.

The only other group which might be considered in this regard is that comprising the jurists of ancient Rome. However, the insights of the jurists were confined to the context of discussion of damages with respect to sales of slave-capital.[3] The Rabbis, by contrast, ranged beyond the question of damages. Further, they employed

---

[1] For a survey of research to the late 1960's, see Mark Blaug (ed.), *Economics and Education* (Baltimore, Md.,: Penguin, 1968). Consult also, R. Wykstra (ed.), *Education and the Economics of Human Capital* (New York: Free Press, 1971).

[2] See, e.g., B.F. Kiker, "The Historical Roots of the Concept of Human Capital", *Journal of Political Economy* (October 1966), pp. 481–99.

[3] Consult, Barry Gordon, *Economic Analysis Before Adam Smith: Hesiod to Lessius* (New York: Barnes and Noble, 1975), pp. 137–139.

human capital concepts in the examination of issues relating to free persons as well as slaves.

There were three main points of departure for Talmudic debate in the field of human capital analysis. One of these was the biblical account, in the *Book of Exodus*, of the construction of the Tabernacle. Another was the problem of estimation of appropriate compensation in cases of physical and psychological injury. A third, involved attempts at the valuation of human life, which attempts were evoked by the section of the *Book of Leviticus* which deals with the dedication of persons to the sanctuary.

A Point of Departure

The term "human capital" refers to the bundle of skills and abilities that an individual brings into a labour market. The contents of the bundle can include such items as native talent, general educational attainment, and specialized vocational skills. The creation and/or development of human capital are supposed to derive from education and training, in the main.[4]

Talmudic scholars were led to enter into consideration of such issues by virtue of the need to reflect on a particular passage of the biblical Book of Exodus. The passage concerned is part of the surviving heritage of ancient Jewish literature, and it pertains to the construction of the Tabernacle (Ex. 35:30–35). It reads:

> . . . Then Moses said unto the children of Israel: See God hath called by name Bezalel . . . And He has filled him with the spirit of God, with wisdom, with insight and with knowledge and with all manner of workmanship. And to combine ideas to work them in gold and silver and copper, and in cutting stones for setting, and in carving wood, in making all kinds of designed work. And also the gift of teaching hath He put in his heart; both he and Ahaliab . . . both He filled with wisdom of heart to do all manner of work of the artist-engraver, of weaver and embroiderer in sky-blue and purple wool, in

---

[4] As a concept, "human capital" is sometimes distinguished from that of "human resources". The latter refers to the size and ability of the *population* available to a society to further that society's goals. It includes elements such as productive capacity, adaptability and reasoning power. Further, there is a noteworthy difference between the commodity approach to "human capital" and the "human resources" approach. Proponents of the former maintain that people work simply because they have to make a living. They consider work a disutility. Whereas, followers of the latter assert that man also derives satisfaction from work in that it is a social function with a multiplicity of goals which contains a measure of utility. Concerning the foregoing, see Eli Ginsberg, *The Human Economy* (New York: McGraw Hill, 1976), pp. VII–XIII, and 3–30.

scarlet-wool and in fine linen, and in general weaving, executing all
manner of work and combining ideas.[5]

Although Christian commentators generally passed over this
passage as mere narrative, talmudists were disposed to be far more
attentive. Detail relating to the Temple was a matter for on-going
research and debate among the latter. Consideration of the implications of the construction of the Tabernacle posed issues about
the acquisition of skill, its application in the form of "productive"
work, and its remuneration. Here was a point of departure for a line
of analysis of phenomena which most of the literate ancients found
beneath notice.

Productive Work

From *Exodus*, the obvious focus for labour input in the Tabernacle
episode is the master-craftsman, Bezalel. According to the analyses
of the talmudic scholars, Bezalel was endowed with three attributes: *Hokhma*, *Tevunah* and *Daat*; "wisdom", "insight", and
"knowledge" which he combined "with all manner of workman-
ship". The Talmud (B'rakhot 55a) in commenting upon Bezalel's
exceptional qualities, makes a very unusual observation ". . . God
does not provide wisdom except to those who already possess it for
it is stated 'He gives wisdom to the wise and understanding to those
who understand . . .'" (Daniel 2:20). And to augment this, the
Talmud continues to show that the same biblical narrative which
tells about Bezalel's artistic abilities and his Divine calling make
this very point: ". . . In the heart of all that are wisehearted, I have
put wisdom" (Exodus 31:6). Thus, wisdom and understanding
require qualities of knowledge and intellectual development, of
character and of intelligence. Here, there is the strong suggestion
that in order to become the recipient of Divine inspiration, one has
first to acquire wisdom by one's own efforts. This appears to have
been the case with Bezalel.

How does one acquire such characteristics in the first place?
According to Rashi[6] *wisdom* is acquired through "learning from
others, through study". *Insight* is the "intelligence to deduce independent ideas from what one has learned." And *knowledge* "comes
from Divine inspiration", which according to biblical teaching is

---

[5] *The Pentateuch*, translated into German by Samson Raphael Hirsch (1867–78)
Vol. II Exod., and rendered into English by Isaac Levy, (London 1956).
[6] See Rashi's explanation on Ex. 31:3. *Rashi* (1040–1105) is considered the
foremost interpreter of the Hebrew Bible and the Talmud.

the ultimate resource in that the human imagination is linked to the human spirit.

The question addressed by Rashi is taken up at a later date by the outstanding 17th century exegete-philosopher, R. Moshe Gentili-Hefez (1663–1711). In his view, learning requires assiduous human effort, whereas the acquisition of knowledge is a product of intellectual growth. Gentili writes:

> True, every human endeavour requires Divine assistance. Still, it is incumbent upon man to cleave to scholars to learn. Indeed, without diligence knowledge will not drop from heaven. For how can one become wise without assiduous effort. Moreover, there are two kinds of skills: one is imitative, the other educative. In the event of the former, one just uses ingenuity to execute his work. The former's work is necessarily imperfect, whereas the latter's is artistic. Bezalel, on account of his educational background, possessed the qualities of the latter. He was steeped in theory and practice, which along with Divine assistance, he implemented creatively and productively.[7]

Gentili entitled his homiletical-philosophical work "Melekhet Mahashevet", i.e., "work resulting from thought". This phrase is taken from the Book of Exodus (35:33), and it is related directly to a variety of passages in cognate literature. For example, the *Talmud*[8] in seeking to identify the various kinds of work forbidden on the Sabbath, deduces analogically that all "work of thought" which took place at the construction of the *Tabernacle* is in the category of "Melekhet Mahashevet", meaning "work resulting from thought". In the view of R. Yehoshua (T. Keritut 19b), such work requires both *Mahashovah* and *Kavanah*, "planning" and "designing", which Rashi interprets to mean "work of thought purposefully executed." Modern Biblical scholars too have defined its meaning in a similar fashion. Thus, Cassuto[9] defines *Melekhet Mahashevet* as "work of thought planned and calculated in advance", and Ch.D. Rabinovitz[10] describes it as "planned work originating in theory and ending in practical application". In either case, the productive element as a result of applied knowledge is evident.

---

[7] See R. Moshe Gentili-Hefez, *Melekhet Mahashevet* (Venice, 1710) p. 105. These extracts were freely translated from Hebrew into English.

[8] See Babyl, Talmud, *Baitza* 13b, *Haigiga*, 10b, *Baba Kama* 26b, *Sanh*, 62b and other Tractates, notably Tractate *Sabbath*, along with Rashi's explanation. See also, *Eglei Tal* (1905) by Abraham Bornstein. It is a study of the laws of the Sabbath.

[9] Cassuto, M.D., *Commentary on Exodus* (Hebrew University of Jerusalem, 1951), p. 321.

[10] Ch. D. Rabinovitz, *Daat Sophrim* on Exodus (Jerusalem, 1963) p. 276.

Return on Investment

While the verses of Exodus encouraged the talmudic scholars to consider productivity as the outcome of investment in human resources, the biblical narrative offered no obvious lead concerning the manner in which "melekhet mahashevet" was to be compensated. Exodus omits any reference to compensation for the artistic and skilful work rendered by Bezalel and his compatriots in the building of the Tabernacle. Despite this omission, the talmudists felt obliged to fill the gap by recourse to other sections of the Scriptures.

According to talmudic tradition, the artisans were paid from a special fund of accumulated capital. The fund was termed *bedek-habayit*, and specifically designated for the repairing of the Temple.[11] The pecuniary award from the *bedek-habayit* fund, was derived by the talmudic scholars inferentially from a verse in Exodus XXV:18, thus linking the terms of payment at the construction of the Temple in Jerusalem to those of the Tabernacle in the wilderness following the Exodus.[12]

The rendition was not done arbitrarily, for there is in fact a corroborating passage in II Kings, XII:10–13, which records how Yehoiada the priest took a chest and bore a hole in the lid of it, and all the money that was donated to the Temple was put into it. With those funds they paid the workmen, the carpenters and the builders "who worked upon the house of the Lord", the masons, and the stonecutters.[13]

Thus, the artisans were paid their salaries in money, but if they desired, they could be paid in goods. However, since the gifts in kind (or assessments) to the *bedek-habayit* fund were deemed "consecrated", they had first to be secularized before they could be used as a form of payment. The process of secularization involved the Temple authorities in a set of transactions. According to the *Tosefta* (edited ca. 200CE), a worker (in the sanctuary) cannot say "I would like to be paid with a cow or with a garment . . .", for anything consecrated cannot be turned into a means of payment *for*

---

[11] See *Shekalim*, Ch.V, Mishnah 6. There was a special chamber in the Temple called "the chamber of *bedek-habayit*" where all the "consecrated" gifts were put.

[12] Tractate *Temurah*, 31b ". . . We infer that we pay from the dedications for the repair of the Temple." [Whence do we derive this?] said R. Abbahu: since scripture says "And let them make *Me* [a Sanctuary], intimating from 'is Mine,' i.e. that monies dedicated for "bedek-habayit" were set aside for the building and repairing the Temple (Transl. The Soncino Press).

[13] See II *Kings*, XII:10–13.

work.[14] Only money may be paid. How then was he compensated? First, an equivalent sum of his salary was set aside. The object in question was subsequently monetized and thereby rendered secular. As a result, the artisan could then receive that good in lieu of his contractually agreed upon compensation. Now, with the money originally set aside, a similar good was purchased from the "chamber of general gifts" and transferred to the *chamber of bedek-habayit*.

What is perhaps most characteristic in this instance, is the complicated procedure of *monetization* and *market transfer* that was used in order to facilitate a commensurate compensation to the artisans for the productive work they carried out at the building and/or repairing of the sanctuary. Hence the Talmudic statement: Notmin Me'hen Le'Umanim Be'skharon (Temurah, 31b), "the artisans were paid commensurate salaries from the originally consecrated goods".

With respect to payments, there was also a distinction between ordinary workers and skilled tradesmen. If one was a *poel*, a hired worker for a specific time period, he was paid the going wage rate from the *bedek-habayit* fund in currency. If one was an *Uman*, a craftsman contracting his job, he was paid from the same fund the contractually agreed upon sum for his specialized work.

Ability and Income

What transpires from the foregoing analysis is essentially an evolutionary process, beginning with education and training whereby wisdom and understanding is acquired. Thereupon, God bestows wisdom to the wise, thus building wisdom upon wisdom resulting in knowledge. All this leads to *Melekhet Mahashevet*, or productive work from which given earnings are derived either in form of wages or agreed upon compensation for a specific task by an expert craftsman. Diagrammatically it may be presented as follows:

The explicit theological dimensions of the above are foreign to contemporary, positivistic economic analysis. However, the Talmudic schema as it developed, embodied the fundamental functional relationships which are affirmed in the human capital literature of current Economics. The talmudic writers posited the existence of strong linkages between education, productivity, and earnings.

---

[14] See *Tosefta, Meilah*, Ch. 1:12. *Tosefta* (Lit., "Additions") is the name of a collection of Talmudic "Baraitot" which treat the subject of traditional laws in a more complete form than does the *Mishnah*. See also, Maimonides (12th cent.), *Avoda, Meilah*, Ch. 8:3–4. The extracts were freely translated by the authors.

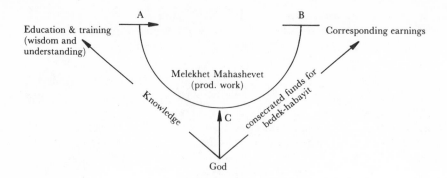

The Value of Human Life

Concern with human capital issues was evoked also by the talmudic investigation of the value of human life. Here, the foundation is
the *Book of Leviticus* which dates from at least the ninth century
B.C.E. and is part of the "priestly" contribution to the Hebrew scriptures. The most relevant passage reads, as follows (Lv. 27:1–8):

> Yahweh spoke to Moses; he said: Speak to the sons of Israel and tell
> them: If anyone vows the value of a person to Yahweh and wishes to
> discharge the vow: a man between twenty and sixty years of age shall
> be valued at fifty silver shekels—the sanctuary shekel; a woman shall
> be valued at thirty shekels; between five and twenty years, a boy shall
> be valued at twenty shekels, a girl at ten shekels; between one month
> and five years, a boy shall be valued at five silver shekels, a girl at
> three silver shekels; at sixty years and over, a man shall be valued at
> fifteen shekels and a woman at ten shekels. If the person who made
> the vow cannot meet this valuation, he must present the person
> concerned to the priest, and the priest shall set a value proportionate
> to the resources of the person who made the vow.

Here, it is clear, persons are classified into four categories by age:
from one month to five years; from five to twenty years; from
twenty to sixty years; and, from sixty years upward. Then, money
values are assigned to each category of person, by sex. The highest
values are set on those aged between twenty and sixty. Younger
persons are given lower values, as are older persons. The schema of
valuation is displayed in the following table:

		Assessed Valuation	
Age		*Male*	*Female*
I.	From one month to five years	5 Shekels	3 Shekels
II.	From five to twenty years	20 "	10 "

III. From twenty to sixty years	50	"	30	"
IV. From sixty and upward	15	"	10	"

What is the rationale of this pattern of valuation? *Leviticus* offers no direct answer to this question, but there are other sections of the Hebrew scriptures which suggest that the rationale was, variation in market value of a person, as if that person were a slave, i.e., a human capital object.

Among the scriptural passages which bear upon the quantifications of *Leviticus* is that relating to the sale of Joseph into slavery by his brothers. *Genesis* states:

> Now some Midianite merchants were passing, and they drew Joseph up out of the well. They sold Joseph to the Ishmaelites for twenty silver pieces, and these men took Joseph to Egypt. (Gen., 37:38).

Joseph, at this time, was clearly older than five and was almost certainly younger than twenty. His price, as a slave, is in direct accord with the *Leviticus* scale.

Further confirmation of the market-slave basis of the *Leviticus* scale for the value of human life is afforded by the episode concerning the prophet Hosea and his adulterous, prostitute wife Gomer. At one point (Ho. 3:2) the prophet buys his wife back, "for fifteen silver shekels and a bushel-and-a-half of barley," and here, the *Interpreter's Bible* comments:

> Gomer was now a slave to the master she served . . . The total price which Hosea paid for Gomer must have been according to this calculation—thirty shekels. And since Exodus 21:32 gives that as the amount of compensation to be paid to the owner for the killing of a slave, it has been calculated that such an amount was a slave's market value and that was the price which Hosea paid.

Thirty shekels (or, fifteen shekels plus the value of the barley) corresponds to the present value of a woman aged between twenty and sixty, according to *Leviticus*.

Given that market value was established in this early literature as the touchstone for setting the price on a person, the Talmudic writers followed up with a variety of refinements on the basic theme. For example, the Rabbis pondered the fact that, in the *Leviticus* scale, when a man reached the age of sixty his value diminished by more than one-third, i.e., from fifty to fifteen shekels. However, the value of a woman declined to one-third only, i.e., from thirty to ten shekels (*Arakhin*, 19a). In the opinion of Hezekiah (third century C.E.), the difference is due to the contrast in the productivities of aged persons. Hezekiah states:

People say, an old man in the house is a liability in the house, while
an old woman in the house is an asset in the house.

Later, Rashi comments that a woman over sixty is still likely to
be able to engage in productive work, whereas a man can be
effective no longer because of his "shever", i.e., his poorer health.[15]
The Talmudic tradition is also concerned to stress the need for
personal viability if any money sum is to be assigned to human
worth. In *Arakhin*, 6b, it is stated that: "One who is at the point of
death or about to be executed cannot have his worth vowed nor be
subject to valuation." With respect to the person about to be
executed, Rashi observes that, "since no one will purchase a con-
demned man, he possesses no market value." As for the dying
person, Maimonides (1135–1204) reasons that, "one who is at the
point of death is just as being dead, and a dead person has neither
an estimated nor a market value."[16] Quantification of the value of
life, then, is contingent on the object's possession of legal and
physical identity as well as on existing market conditions.

Compensation for Injury

Yet another point of departure for Talmudic concern with human
capital issues is provided by the debates on questions regarding
compensation for injury. The relevant discussion, which is located
mainly in the section called *Nezikin* (Damages), has a consistently
quantitative dimension in that it attempts to assign monetary forms
of compensation. Market evaluations are employed to help establish the economic worth of the human capital involved. As with the
debates stemming from the dedication of persons to the sanctuary,
the prices of slaves are prominent points of reference. Again, this
area of discussion has its roots in biblical prescriptions concerning
damages.
From the viewpoint of the modern economist, two of the most
striking features of the biblical law codes are the roles assigned to
monetary recompense and to productivity potential when questions
of damages are addressed. The role of money is exemplified in the
following:

---

[15] Rashi, *Arakhin*, 19a. On this issue, Chaim Rabinovitz observes: "Ordinarily
the value of a man is higher than that of a woman. But at old age the opposite is
true, for then a man's value continually declines." *Daat Sophrim*, Erz. edition,
Jerusalem (New York, 1962), p. 307.
[16] Maimonides, *Arakhin u' Kharamin*, Ch. 1:13.

> When a man leaves a pit uncovered, or when he digs one but does not cover it, should an ox, or donkey, fall into it, then the owner of the pit shall make up for the loss: he must pay its owner money, and the dead animal shall be his own. (Ex. 21:33–34).

Sums of money are also crucial in the case of the violation of a virgin. The relevant passage reads: "If a man seduces a virgin who is not bethrothed and sleeps with her, he must pay her price (i.e., the bride-price, or *mohar*) and make her his wife. If her father absolutely refuses to let him have her, the seducer must pay a sum of money equal to the price fixed for a virgin." (Ex. 22:15–17).

Other examples can be cited, and, as various biblical scholars have shown, similar provisions of assessing fines for damages or rape existed among the advanced Semitic nations in the Near-East. The Code of Hammurabi, the Hittite and the Assyrian laws, as well as the Pentateuchal civil laws, reveal a remarkable similarity, sometimes even in their very phrasing of those laws. Thus, in the Assyrian law, "rape was treated precisely in the same way, except that the price was three times the normal marriage price" (Interpreter's Bible, p. 1006). The same holds true of the Babylonian principle of making restitution for damages. And the same custom prevailed anciently with respect to the *Mohar*. (Driver, p. 229.)[17]

The role of productivity emerges strongly on a number of occasions, and, most notably, where damages to land are involved. Hence, the Code of the Covenant affirms:

> When a man puts his animals out to graze in another's field, he must make restitution for the part of the field that has been grazed in proportion to its yields. But if he has let the whole field be grazed, he must make restitution in proportion to the best crop recorded in the injured party's field or vineyard. (Ex. 22:4–5)

Further, loss of productivity by persons due to "enforced inactivity" is also envisaged as ground for compensation. The relevant passage reads: "If men quarrel and one strikes the other a blow with stone or fist so that the man though he does not die, must keep his bed, the one who struck the blow shall not be liable provided the other gets up and can go about, even with a stick. He must compensate him, however, for his enforced inactivity, and care for him until he is completely cured." (Ex. 21:18–19).

Informed with these insights on the significance of productivity and on the social role of money, the contributors to the *Talmud*

---

[17] See, J.H. Herz, *The Pentateuch* (London, 1958), Exod., pp. 312, 403, Deut. 843; *Interpreters Bible* (Nashville: Abingdon Press, 1956), p. 1006; S.R. Driver, op. cit., p. 229.

reasoned in terms of five categories of indemnity for damaged free persons. As established in the *Mishna* (B.K. 83b–85ff.) the relevant categories are: *Nezek* ("depreciation"); *Tzar* ("pain"); *Repoi* ("healing"); *Shevet* ("loss of time"); and, *Boshet* ("degradation"). Considered together, the categories offer a basis for a comprehensive approach to indemnification which takes account of such factors as the health, age, mental capacity, and type of productive employment of the person concerned. Evaluation requires the application of a variety of criteria.

In a recent analysis of the *Talmud's* treatment of compensation for personal injury, the author has observed that economic reasoning is not employed consistently to establish the grounds for damages in all five categories. This is most evident in the case of "degradation", which may also be translated as "indignity", "insult" or "humiliation." Here, market values are not invoked, but rather the social standing of the offender and the aggrieved.[18] As the *Talmud* puts it:

> ha-kol l'fee hamebayesh v'hamitvayesh (i.e., "all according to the social position of the insulter and the insulted." Baba Kama. 83b).

Accordingly, it is in the instance of *physical* damage—an eye, an arm, a leg—where there is a monetary loss ("hissaron—kis")—that recourse is had to a person's loss of market value. Where "psychic" damage, such as humiliation is involved, the analogy breaks down and is not pursued. However, as has been pointed out, the reason for this is, "because of the difficulty in measuring *boshet* in monetary terms . . ." (Encycl. Judaica, 1972).[19]

Though there is no obvious lead in the *Talmud* as to why "degradation" is not assessed in the same manner as the other four items, the reason for this distinction is well grounded in the very characteristics of this item. Alternately, "depreciation", "healing" and "loss of time", are categories which readily lend themselves to market evaluations. Even "pain", which is an "invisible" injury, because of its physical dimension can be subject of a sort of "pain-pleasure calculus", albeit in a theoretical market. Not so "shame", which is indicative of an emotional state of mind. It must have been obvious to the Talmudic master logicians, that for psychic feelings of hurt, not even a hypothetical market can be postulated. To put it

---

[18] E. Kleiman, "Opportunity Cost, Human Capital, and some Related Economic Concepts in Talmudic Literature", *History of Political Economy*, 19:2 (1987), pp. 263–285.

[19] See, *Encyclopedia Judaica*, "Damages" (Keter Publ., 1972) p. 1234.

in the modern idiom: no "utility index" can be projected for moods. Hence, their non-pursual of the market analogy, which would have been pointless.[20]

"Healing" (or, "doctor's bills") is an element of compensation which poses fewer analytical problems than the foregoing, although the Rabbis perceive that the financial obligation on the offender to meet the medical expenses of the injured party can be complicated by strategems which either may adopt. The fourth element, "loss of time" or "inactivity" is related directly to the productivity-based consideration which was recognised in *Exodus* 21:18–19 (quoted above). The idea is that there are foregone opportunities resulting from involuntary unemployment of human capital because of a period of enforced convalescence.[21] Payment for the loss of opportunities is due in the form of a fixed sum levy.

Finally, there is "depreciation" (or, "damage"). This element represents recognition that a particular physical injury may not result merely in a period of temporary involuntary unemployment. The injury may also involve a permanent loss of human capital, and hence, a continuing short-fall in future earnings as compared with those that could have been anticipated before the injury. Quantification of this aspect of compensation by the *Talmud's* contributors and by later commentators is of special interest in terms of subsequent economic thought.

Rashi, Rosh, and Depreciation

The basic text in the *Mishna* concerning depreciation (or, damage) reads, as follows:

> If he put out his eye, cut off his arm or broke his leg, the injured person is considered as if he were a slave being sold in the market place, and an evaluation is made as to how much he was worth (previously) and as to how much he is worth (now). (B.K. 83b).

---

[20] The fact that the *Mishnah* established "pain" and "shame" as two distinct categories (even though pain can also be mental) is a clear indication that its authors viewed these two items from two different perspectives—the physical and the emotional, with the application of economic values to the former and social values to the latter. For comparison, see Anastasios D. Karayiannis' interesting article, "Democritus on Ethics and Economics", *Rivista Internazionale Di Scienze Economiche e Commerciali*, Vol. XXXV, No. 4–5, Milano, Italy, (April–May 1988), pp. 379–80, about Democritus' notion concerning the measurability of psychic feelings of pleasure and pain.

[21] The role of foregone opportunities in talmudic thought was first discussed some twenty years ago in, R.A. Ohrenstein, "Economic Thought in Talmudic Literature in the Light of Modern Economics", *American Journal of Economics and Sociology*, 27 (1968), pp. 187–90.

Immediately, it is apparent that here the labour of a free man is to be equated with that of a slave, for the purpose of the exercise in hand. This type of equation, it can be noted, is entirely in accord with the traditional Jewish treatment of the value of human life (as noted above). Money sums applied to persons whose values were vowed to God are in direct correspondence with traditional evalua- tion of classes of slaves, by age and sex. Further, the equation finds support in some of the economic thought of much later centuries. For example, in his, *An Outline of the Science of Political Economy* (1836), the first Drummond Professor of Political Economy at Oxford University wrote:

> The only differences . . . between a freeman and a slave are, first that the freeman sells himself, and only for a period, and to a certain extent the slave may be sold by others, and absolutely; and, secondly, that the personal qualities of the slave are a portion of the wealth of his master; those of the freeman, so far as they can be made the subject of exchange, are a part of his own wealth.[22]

In addition to the slave-freeman equation, the Mishanic text indicates that for the early Rabbis it was reasonable, for some purposes, to argue in terms of an analogous relationship between human capital and physical capital in as much as both may be subject to depreciation.[23] The Mishanic text also suggests that justice requires an estimation of the present market value of a person's future expected earnings.[24]

On and beyond the *Talmud* proper there is the work of definitive commentators including Rashi (1040–1105) and R. Asher b. Yehiel, who is known as Rosh (1250–1327). With these medieval scholars, the anticipation of the modern capitalized-earning proce-

---

[22] Nassau W. Senior, *An Outline of the Science of Political Economy* (1836, Kelley, New York, 1965) p. 10.

[23] The analogy is also employed in the modern literature dealing with life insurance. See, e.g., S.S. Huebner, *The Economics of Life Insurance* (3rd ed., New York: Appleton-Century Crofts, 1955), pp. 21–22.

[24] Although this principle is presented in general terms, its economic dimen- sions are elaborated upon in the *Amoraic* discussions (Talmud proper), or by successive generations of commentators. One such discourse, though in a different context, will illustrate the point. It pertains to a biblical passage in *Leviticus* 25:47–53. To avoid the intricacies of the debate and for the sake of brevity, it will suffice to point out that the question revolves around the method of calculating the value of a Hebrew slave in the event of his redemption before the conclusion of his term of service. Specifically, is the amount to be refunded to the purchaser based merely on the slave's original price, (i.e., his purchasing price minus the time period he already served), or is the calculation based on his *current* market value, and, therefore, subject to changing market conditions of "ups" and "downs", his "state of health and strength" and on variations in his productive capacity; "improved" or "deteriorating" performance? (Kidd. 20a–b, Arakh. 30b).

dure for the determination of the value of human capital emerges with greater clarity. Controversy concerning which kind of slave provided the relevant market criterion for evaluation offers a basis for appreciation of the modernity of the Talmudic tradition with respect to this aspect of economic analysis.

According to Rashi, evaluation of indemnity for human depreciation should be based on the market value of a Hebrew slave. Rosh disagrees with this. The assessment should be calculated in terms of the market value of a non-Hebrew slave. Such a dispute, it can be appreciated, is a quite radical one if the profound difference between the two categories of slave in terms of Scriptural legislation is also appreciated. Both *Exodus* and *Deuteronomy* require the release of Hebrew slaves from bondage after six years of service (Ex. 21:1–2; Dt. 15:12–13). No such requirement applies to non-Hebrew human capital. In fact, the latter, "shall be your property and you may leave them as an inheritance to your sons after you, to hold in perpetual possession. These you may have for slaves; but to your brothers, the sons of Israel, you must not be hard masters."(Lv. 25:45–46).

The character of the dispute between Rashi and Rosh provides the strongest type of confirmation that in the Talmudic tradition the present economic value of a person was regarded as a variable dependent upon expectation of the future stream of labour services which was likely to be forthcoming. Otherwise, why dispute whether or not a Hebrew or non-Hebrew slave should be the point of market reference? Clearly, the non-Hebrew slave criterion (given equality of age, health, and sex) yielded a much more generous award for "damage" than its alternate, since the flow of labour services would be untrammelled by sabbatical (or, it can be added, Jubilee) considerations.

This notion was crystallized even further by R. Nathan Spira (16th cent.) in a gloss on R. Isaac Alfasi, known as RIF (1013–1103). He writes that even according to Rashi the same method of capitalization of expected earnings can also be applied to a Hebrew slave, simply by calculating his anticipated productive employment throughout his lifetime by means of six-year units: "You assess the Hebrew slave's value as if he initially sells himself for six years. Upon completion of his first term, he sells himself for another six years. Thereupon, he repeats the same for another six years, until his death, according to the life expectancy of a person". (Alfasi, B.K. p. 30a).

Conclusion

As the foregoing analysis illustrates, the Rabbinic discussion of compensation for injury, like the examination of the worth of human life, evoked attention to the concept of the present value of a person and to the problem of measuring that value.[25] Writers in the Talmudic tradition looked to calculations regarding expected income flow from the labour of the valuee as the best approach to measurement. Further, these writers were keenly aware that the idea of the existence of capital in persons implied the notion of a process of investment in those persons. With respect to this latter, it is entirely in character that the *Talmud Jerusalem* relates the following exchange between two distinguished scholars. When R. Hama b. Hanina visited the Assembly Houses in Lod (Palestine) he was moved to exclaim: "Look, how much money my ancestors have invested here!" However, R. Hoshiah the Great retorted: "Say, how much money have your ancestors invested in people? Were not there many people who needed an education (in the Torah)?" (*Sh'kalim*, V:15, a–b).

---

[25] The Rabbinic treatment of the value of human life also relates to economic issues beyond the bounds of human capital theory. On those issues, see, Roman A. Ohrenstein, "Value Analysis in Talmudic Literature in the Light of Modern Economics," *International Journal of Social Economics*, Vol. 13, No. 3 (1986), incorporating the *International Review of Economics and Ethics*, Vol. 1, No. 1 (1986), pp. 34–53.

PART FIVE

IMPACT ON WESTERN ECONOMICS

CHAPTER TEN

JEWS IN THE EUROPEAN ECONOMY

In the foregoing chapters we have demonstrated a deal of the rich array of talmudic concepts and lines of analysis which were to re-emerge in the development of modern economic thought. However, the explorations in Chapters Three to Nine were mainly retrospective in character. They did not address the issue of whether or not aspects of talmudic thought may have had an impact in Europe such that seeds were sown to bear fruit later as Economics began to emerge as a distinct discipline. This latter issue is a vast one which has been little considered by historians of economic ideas. Such is the state of scholarship in this field that only preliminary observations are possible at this stage. Nevertheless, there are strong grounds for pursuing the issue, and some of those grounds are considered in this concluding chapter.

Until the thirteenth century, most Jewish people lived in regions where Islamic culture was predominant. Thereafter, Jews became increasingly prominent in areas of Europe, at first in the South and later in the North. In some of those areas, and for lengthy periods, Jewish communities experienced a good measure of toleration. Salo Baron writes:

> Not only orally but often in widely circulating pamphlets and treatises, the Jews were in a position to discuss frankly the differences between their own and the Christian attitude to life. In few modern countries . . . would men be allowed to speak their minds so freely and in a way so clearly running counter to the established order and the interests of its dominant group.[1]

By the time of the crusades, this situation had altered in many regions. However, given the periods of dialogue, and given the prominent role of Jews in trade and finance, it seems most probable that European economic thought and practice came to be influenced by Jewish understanding and custom.

---

[1] S.W. Baron, *Ancient and Medieval Jewish History* (New Brunswick: Rutgers University Press, 1972), p. 266.

Usury and the Jews

History suggests that none but the most rudimentary economic system can endure for any length of time under conditions in which a price for the use of money is inhibited. Where, for example, the taking of interest is outlawed, a price for money emerges in other forms. This is illustrated by recent developments in certain Islamic nations. Timur Kuran observes:

> As in the past, it is proving difficult to implement some of Islam's perceived economic requirements. A case in point is the ban on interest, which constitutes the *raison d'etre* of the Islamic banks that have mushroomed throughout North Africa, the Middle East, South Asia, and elsewhere. The banks have eliminated interest only in name: they use a panoply of practices that can only be characterised as interest in Islamic garb. Although the matter is shrouded in controversy, a number of Islamic economists have sought to legitimize these practices.[2]

An analogous ban pertained in most parts of Europe during the early and high middle ages. Roman law tradition allowed for interest payment in two types of real contract. One of these contracts was *depositum irregulare*. The other was *mutuum*, a loan for consumption, if the *mutuum* was linked to a second, verbal contract known as *stipulatio*.[3] The Justinian Code set a maximum interest rate of 12.5 per cent per annum for most loans. In the case of loans to farmers, the maximum allowable was 4.5 per cent. On the other hand, the Canon law tradition forbade interest-taking, and this ban was extended into civil law by the Emperor Charlemagne (C.E. 742–814). The very general condemnation of interest-taking in law at this time constituted the cornerstone of subsequent medieval usury legislation.[4] Such legislation became more severe and prohibitive over the next five hundred years. Only in late medieval and renaissance Europe were theologians and jurists to establish legitimate grounds for the receipt of interest.

With Christians under strong moral and legal pressure to deny themselves income by way of interest, there was an understandable restriction in the supply of loanable funds. Hence, it proved convenient on economic grounds to tolerate, and even encourage, the presence of a group in the community which could undertake

---

[2] S. Todd Lowry (ed.), *Pre-Classical Economic Thought* (Boston: Kluwer, 1987), p. 111.

[3] For detail, see, B. Gordon, *Economic Analysis Before Adam Smith* (London: Macmillan, 1975), pp. 135–9.

[4] C.f., J.T. Noonan, *The Scholastic Analysis of Usury* (Cambridge, Mass.: Harvard University Press, 1957), p. 15.

certain of the financial functions denied the majority. Jews were able to fulfil the role required in clear conscience because of the different legal tradition to which they were heirs. The outcomes of long talmudic debate, based on the realities of Eastern economies, allowed observant Jewish businessmen a scope which Canon law edicts, based on the less sophisticated economies of the Western Roman Empire in decline, could not comprehend.[5]

The legal tradition of the Jews on usury was grounded in the original biblical injunctions which prohibited interest-taking only on loans amongst Jews. Interest could be demanded of foreigners. The reason for this was that the foreigner in mind was usually a businessman who borrowed money for commercial purposes in the expectation of profit. The Jew in mind was a farmer (the economy of ancient Israel was agricultural and pastoral) who borrowed for purposes of consumption. Such borrowing by agriculturalists often led to disastrous consequences including expropriation of assets and enslavement. Another consideration was that, whereas Israelites were in no position to forbid foreigners to demand interest on loans, it would have been an affront to national solidarity for a Jew to grant a foreigner a cheap loan which he in turn could re-lend at profit to another Jew.

As the economic circumstances of the Jewish people altered, particularly the circumstances of those who prospered by exile in Babylon, so the law regarding usury changed. Talmudic scholars made a clear distinction between loans for consumption, on the one hand, and the granting of credit for productive purposes. The rabbis prohibited all money lending at interest both to Jew and Gentile alike when the loan was intended to meet consumption needs.[6] However, when credit was extended for reasons of productive gain, the talmudists began to find means whereby there could be a return to the lender in excess of the principal of the loan.

At a period when the expansion of the Persian economy required greater facilities for credit, Babylonian rabbis legalized the practice of antichretic sales. This allowed Jews to evade the prohibition of usury under the guise of fictitious exchanges.[7] Concerning this

---

[5] The regression of the Roman economy from c. 193 (during the reign of the pre-Christian Emperor Septimus Severus) is discussed in, B. Gordon, *The Economic Problem in Biblical and Patristic Thought* (Leiden and New York: E.J. Brill, 1989), pp. 92–7.

[6] *Baba Mezia*, 69a. Babylonian tradition was opposed to lending at interest to a Gentile. See, *Babylonian Talmud*, B.M., 70b: San. 25b, Mak. 24a.

[7] Consult, Boaz Cohen, *Antichresis in Jewish and Roman Law* (New York, 1950), pp. 179–202. See also, *Talmud Kethuboth* 86a, and *Kiddushin*, 47.

innovation, Salo Baron comments that, "since Jews were in the front rank of merchants and bankers in the generally backward empire, it would seem that it was they who set the pace in developing such new commercial policies".[8] Such innovatory activity, it can be remarked, was a harbinger of Jewish commercial initiative in medieval Europe (see below).

One of the devices associated with the rabbinic sanctioning of antichretic sales by Babylonian Jews was the so-called *Tarsha*, or, "deaf interest". This allowed one to charge more than the proper price for a commodity in exchange for an extension of the payment date.[9] Another method was the *suran* note or mortgage, which allowed the debtor to mortgage his field to the creditor for a stipulated time at the end of which it reverted to the debtor without payment.[10] Still another legal device was a mortgage with fixed, annual deductions wherein the creditor took possession of the debtor's property and deducted the usufruct from the debt.[11]

On and beyond these, the most important legal fiction that permitted usurious loans (and one that was to become widespread in Christian Europe) was the so-called *Iska*, or *Commenda* contract. This was a partnership arrangement wherein the creditor agreed to share in both the profits and losses of the venture.[12] In Europe, by the age of the scholar Maimonides (12th century) these *Commenda* contracts were widely regarded as legitimate business arrangements. With the growth of international Jewish commerce, they became of vital importance since they enabled merchants to entrust consignments of merchandise to fellow Jews travelling to foreign lands. Usually, it was the practice that after the disposal of these goods abroad, the creditor got back the invested capital plus a stipulated share of the profit.[13] Obviously, with such a device at hand, the prohibition of usury could be evaded easily.

The *Commenda* contract's use became well entrenched in medieval international trade. Christian merchants followed their Jewish counterparts in adopting the device. As such, it is one of the most prominent, but by no means unique, examples of the manner in which talmudic commercial law provided a model for orderly eco-

---

[8] S.W. Baron, *A Social and Religious History of the Jews*, Vol. I (New York, 1952), p. 414.
[9] B.M., 65a.
[10] B.M., 64b.
[11] B.M., 67b.
[12] B.M., 63b, 64a, 70a.
[13] S.W. Baron, *The Economic Views of Maimonides* (New York, 1941), p. 170. See also, ibid., pp. 127–264. Another relevant discussion is, Jacob Katz, *Tradition and Crises* (Jerusalem, 1958).

nomic intercourse which a blanket prohibition of usury would seem to forbid.

Innovation and High Finance

The Hebrew Bible, in addition to being regarded as the "immutable word of God", was also understood by Jews as the ancient history of their people—spiritual, political, and economic. Since it had always been considered as "The Law of Life", as life's conditions changed the original injunctions of the Bible became subject to interpretation and re-interpretation. The reason for such subjection is grounded in the Jewish understanding of the Law itself. As expounded in the *Talmud*, and in subsequent medieval Jewish literature, the Law is called "Halakha", the root of which is *Ha-Lokh* meaning "to walk", to be in motion, like a river in constant flow (c.f., Chapter One). In short, the Law is a complex system of both tradition and change.

This elastic attitude equipped the Jews with a strong sense of history. Eventually, they became the embodiments of a symbiosis. The latter consisted of a highly developed historical consciousness, intellectual flexibility and physical mobility which, together with "mother necessity", gave them a certain advantage in responding to new economic complexities. It might also be contended that the flexibility was in part due to the fact that Jews were often obliged to live on the margin of societies in which they found themselves. Hence, they were not tied down to the old habits of thought and customary practices of contemporary *milieu*. In consequence, Jews were often freer and braver in discarding accepted notions and in adopting newer and revolutionary concepts. This predisposition may, on occasions, have led to social and scientific breakthroughs.[14]

After an initial period of toleration, Jews in medieval Europe were increasingly marginalized, from about the time of the first crusade. Their economic freedoms became more and more circumscribed. Whereas they had been able to own land and farm it, this avenue of economic activity was increasingly denied them. In addition, they came to be excluded from a variety of commercial endeavours, with Christian merchants moving in to fill the vacuum, and, it should be noted, adopting many of the practices based on the talmudic guidelines of their predecessors.

---

[14] Thorstein Veblen, among others, has argued for this latter contention, most notably in his essay, "Intellectual Pre-eminence of Jews in Modern Europe." See, *The Portable Veblen*, ed. Max Lerner (New York, 1950), pp. 467–79.

The marginalization of European Jewry, as Max Weber and others have pointed out, was not exclusive to Jews in recent centuries. Christian minorities including the Huguenots in France, the Quakers in England, and the Poles in Russia came to be subject to similar pressure. As with the Jews, it would appear that such minorities were driven with peculiar force into economic activity.[15] Probably, marginalization of medieval Jews was often more radical than analogous undertakings, in that attempts were made to deny them public office; invalidate marriages between Christians and Jews; establish ghettos; and, demand that Jews groom and dress themselves in distinctive fashion.[16] If intensity of engagement in economic pursuits is a function of degree of marginalization, then Jews had very strong grounds for single-minded concentration on commercial success.

For some, success was forthcoming, but many of the most prominent medieval Jewish businessmen found themselves placed in the position of obtaining the official protection of the politically powerful at the price of public detestation. Jews were used as convenient tools to effect the processes which the authorities recognized privately as legitimate, but were unprepared to sanction publicly. Popes, bishops, kings and princes readily availed themselves of the services of Jewish financiers. These were engaged to bolster the economies involved. They were also engaged as agents who could undertake activities which would condemn their principals to hellfire and damnation if those principals were personally involved in the mechanics of the activities.

An example of the way in which Jewish businessmen could be exploited by the powerful in the high middle ages is afforded by the case of the British financier, Aaron of Lincoln (C.E., 1125–1186). Aaron's career, "illustrates the manner in which the medieval Jewish communities could be organised into a banking association reaching throughout an entire country, while the ultimate fate of the wealth thus acquired (Henry II seized his property) shows that in the last resort the state was the arch-usurer and obtained the chief benefit from Jewish usury."[17] Expulsion of Jewish bankers,

---

[15] Consult, M. Weber, *General Economic History* (Glencoe, Illinois, 1955), pp. 358–60. See also, Cecil Roth, *Short History of the Jewish People* (London, 1953), pp. 204–5.

[16] Consult, e.g., Kazimierz Kowalski, *The Jewish Question in the Middle Ages According to St. Thomas Aquinas* (Warsaw, 1938), pp. 12–25.

[17] *The Jewish Encyclopedia*, pp. 16–7.

once they had served their purpose in financing the powerful, was not confined to England.[18]

In such climates of uncertainty, Jews were obliged to be in constant readiness to pick themselves up and look for alternate "hosts" and/or "benefactors". One of the effects of the enforced mobility was to encourage a cosmopolitan outlook which helped place some Jews at the centre of international economic activity. In addition, the very dangers which Jews sensed and encountered forced them to mobilize all their capacities to see and say, to dream and plan, to organize and implement, in new ways. As a result, they contributed to the growth and sophistication of international business dealings, and to an increased appreciation of the workings of interactive markets.

Capitalism and the Jews

The origins and causes of modern European capitalism have been much debated by historians, and some of these have proposed links between developments in organized religion and the emergence of capitalist phenomena on a large scale. The best-known thesis in this respect is that expounded by Max Weber who argued that Protestantism, especially in its Puritan form, had a decisive influence in shaping the "spirit of capitalism", and therefore, on the formation of capitalism itself. According to this view, there is a definite cause and effect relationship between the Protestant Reformation and modern capitalism.[19]

Weber's argument has been the subject of considerable controversy over the years.[20] However, it is not our intention here to survey the many ramifications of that controversy. Rather, we wish to remark on the fact that in the course of the debate some of the contributors, in contrast to Weber, have sought to emphasize the role of Jews in the emergence of capitalism.

One of the most notable historians to stress the Jewish factor was Werner Sombart who was particularly impressed by the

---

[18] C.f., Gilbert S. Rosenthal, *Banking and Finance Among Jews in Renaissance Italy* (New York, 1962), pp. 5–7.

[19] Weber's thesis was presented in two papers, "Die protestantische Ethic und der Geist der Kapitalismus", which appeared in the *Archiv fuer Socialwissenschaft und Social-politic* in 1904–5.

[20] On Weber and his critics, see, Roman A. Ohrenstein, "Economic Aspects of Organized Religion: Perspective and Analysis of the Modern Phase", *Nassau Review*, Vol. 2 (Spring 1971), pp. 37–61.

sophisticated character of the economic analysis of the *Talmud*. Sombart wrote that, "some rabbis speak as though they had mastered Ricardo and Marx, or to say the least, they had been brokers on the Stock Exchange or counsel in many an important money-lending case."[21] He went on to claim that what is called "Puritan" by Weber, and others, in the underlying ethos of capitalism is, in reality, "Judaism".

Sombart, like Weber, held that modern capitalism is indeed the product of a specific "Capitalist Spirit"—a condition which did not exist in the Middle Ages. Sombart believed that modern capitalism had a "spirit" of its own which was new in history. That spirit involved unshackled amassing of assets, and profit seeking which paid scant regard to social consequences or interpersonal relations.[22] In the medieval scheme of things, he argued, economic activity was based on the pursuit of the satisfaction of consumer need, whereas modern capitalistic life is impelled by the pursuit of gain (*Bedarfsdeckung* versus *Erwerbsprinzip*).[23] At the basis of this pursuit of gain there is an ethic that is more properly designated as Judaic than Puritan.[24] This thesis concerning the Judaic foundations of European capitalism is extended subsequently to include America. Of the United States, Sombart wrote, ". . . as the golden thread in the tapestry, so are the Jews interwoven as a distinct thread throughout the fabric of American economic history, through the intricacy of their fantastic design it received from the very beginning a pattern all its own."[25]

A number of Jewish scholars have attacked Sombart's thesis.[26] Salo Baron, for one, finds the thesis "brilliant" but "undisciplined". According to Baron, the identification of modern capitalism with "the spirit of Judaism" is "false and profoundly misleading."[27] Further, Sombart himself diminished the creditability of his argument in his later writings. Jacob Oser comments:

> It is interesting to note that Sombart assigned to the Jews a decisive role not only in the development of capitalism, but also in socialism. Early in his life, when he leaned towards Marxism and was critical of

---

[21] W. Sombart, *The Jews and Modern Capitalism* (London, 1913), pp. 313–4.
[22] W. Sombart, *The Quintessence of Capitalism* (New York, 1915), pp. 236–62.
[23] W. Sombart, *Der Modernen Kapitalismus* (Leipzig, 1902).
[24] *The Jews and Modern Capitalism*, p. 41.
[25] ibid., pp. 191–2. C.f., Nathan Glazer, *The Characteristics of American Jews* (New York, 1965), p. 42.
[26] See, e.g., Nathan Reich "Capitalism and the Jews", *The Menorah Journal*, XIII (January, 1930).
[27] S.W. Baron, "Capitalism and the Jewish Fate", *The Menorah Journal*, XXX (July–September, 1942), pp. 120, 137.

capitalism, Sombart emphasized the role of Jews in the development of *capitalism*. After World War I when he developed a strong antipathy toward Marxian Socialism, he found that *socialism* was strongly influenced by Jewish thought."[28]

Undoubtedly, Jews in Europe contributed a good deal to the transition from medieval feudalism to nationalistic mercantilism. This latter involved expansion of the power of central state authority at the expense of more localized rule, and Jews facilitated this trend by loans (sometimes enforced) to central authorities as well as by direct taxation payments which swelled kingly coffers.[29] Secondly, Jews helped weaken the economic dominance of the monopolistic feudal guild structures from which they were excluded. Thirdly, Jews introduced an element of economic liberalism into the "contained" economies of medieval Europe. That liberalism stemmed partly from the necessities of their struggle for economic survival. However, it was also due to their adherence to the *Talmud* and its laws concerning economic behaviour. Those laws had been "basically formulated under the semicapitalist civilization of the Hellenistic and early Roman Empires."[30] The liberal orientation which this initial economic background provided was retained in the talmudic tradition over the centuries.

Given that mercantilist doctrine and practice represents the economics of early capitalism, considerations such as the above suggest that Weber underestimated the role of Jews in the rise of the new economic order. As Gerhard Lenski writes:

> Whether one accepts or rejects Weber's view that Judaism was incapable of generating the modern capitalist system, it seems clear that the Jewish sub-culture greatly facilitates the rise of individuals in an established capitalist system.[31]

On the other hand, it would seem that Sombart overstated the case. Modern capitalism cannot be designated as simply Jewish in inspiration. Jews were capitalism's "putty as well as its moulders." They, "helped to shape the destiny of capitalism, but capitalism also shaped the destiny of Jews."[32]

---

[28] J. Oser, *The Evolution of Economic Thought* (New York, 1963), pp. 161–2.
[29] C.f., S.W. Baron, *Ancient and Medieval Jewish History*, p. 251.
[30] ibid., p. 252.
[31] G. Lenski, *The Religious Factor* (Garden City, New York, 1963), p. 114.
[32] H.M. Sachar, *The Course of Modern Jewish History* (Cleveland and New York, 1958), pp. 39ff.

The Spanish Connection

The preceding sections of this chapter offer considerable evidence that Jews in Europe were in a position to make an impact on the course of the development of Western economic thought. Talmudic law permitted Jews to engage in financial activities which challenged traditional Christian understandings of what was legitimate in this sphere. Again, Jewish appreciation of the character of the Scriptures, plus the social discrimination experienced by Jews, encouraged them to be flexible and cosmopolitan with respect to business practice. They were obliged to be innovatory; at times, on an international scale. In addition they played a significant role in the process of transition from medievalism to modern capitalism.

Despite the above, there has been little systematic investigation by historians of ideas regarding the aspects of talmudic economic thought which may have entered the Western mainstream. Neither, has there been any great progress in identifying the times, places and personalities which may have been involved. It is the purpose of this section to suggest that attention to currents of thought in medieval and renaissance Spain might yield dividends in terms of research on the transmission of economic ideas from Jews to the wider European community.

In medieval Spain, Jews lived under both Christian and Moslem rule. Despite occasional persecutions, many Jews prospered, occupied positions of power, and were widely accepted in secular professional ranks. As early as 948 C.E., a rabbinical school was established at Cordova, and there were notable developments subsequently. From 1104, the academy at Lucena was directed by the celebrated Alfasi (Isaac ben Jacob, of Fez), and later by Joseph ben Migash. Even more celebrated are the contributions of the Cordovan-born scholar Maimonides (1135–1204).[33] Later talmudic authorities to work in Spain included, Asher ben Yehiel of Cologne (1250–1327); Jacob ben Asher (d. 1340); and, Solomon ben Abraham ben Adret (d.1310). Prominent in the output of these scholars were collections of *responsa*, i.e. answers to queries on doubtful points of Jewish law, including law relating to economic behaviour. After the expulsion of the Jews from Spain in 1492, much of this material was summarized by R. Jose Caro of Toledo (1481–1575)

---

[33] Maimonides was the greatest Jewish medieval jurist and philosopher. He wrote extensively on economic subjects. For a survey of his economic thought, see, S.W. Baron, op. cit., pp. 149–235.

in his *Shulhan' Aruk* which became a standard textbook.[34]

Given this distinguished intellectual tradition, the prominence of many Jews in a variety of walks of life, and the opportunities for cultural interpenetration over long periods, it would be surprising if Jewish economic thought and practice failed to have an impact on society at large. One illustration of that impact is provided in the writings on usury of the Catalonian, Saint Raymond of Penafort (1180–1278) who became general of the Dominican Order in 1238. Saint Raymond spent most of his life in Barcelona, a bustling port-city which was a centre of Jewish culture, and when he analyses usurious practices among Christians, he rehearses the very same grounds that were entirely familiar to Spanish rabbis of much earlier days.[35]

Subsequently, cultural interpenetration in Spain was intensified by the increasing persecution which led many Spanish Jews to convert (at least, nominally) to Christianity. These converts, many of whom were engaged in finance and commerce, remained in their existing avocations and continued to observe the long-standing guidelines for commercial intercourse which the Spanish talmudic tradition had established. Hence, traditional talmudic understanding of economic practice persisted in Spain after the expulsion of the Jews, and into the mercantilist era. It is noteworthy too that some of the descendants of the Jewish converts became prominent Christian churchmen and intellectuals. Another element in the cultural inter-mix of Spain, by the fifteenth century, was the long-standing Islamic influence in certain regions. Probably, certain of the conventions concerning trade and commerce in some of those regions still owed more to the *Koran* than they did to the *Talmud* or the Christian developments of Roman and Canon law.

At the very point historically at which the Iberian Peninsula encapsulated a probably unique blend of traditions of economic thought—Jewish, Islamic, and Christian-Spain was subject to an economic revolution, the dimensions of which had no parallel in the West and irrevocably changed the course of economic history. Spain penetrated South America and raped it of those minerals that were regarded as "precious". The resulting inflow of metal, given the monetary conventions which had persisted from Antiquity, led to unprecedented inflationary pressures in Spain and an

---

[34] The above is from, M. Grice-Hutchinson, *Early Economic Thought in Spain, 1177–1704* (London: Allen and Unwin, 1978), pp. 18–9.
[35] ibid, pp. 33–6.

economic decline which challenged all the age-old ideas concerning the means whereby a state could aggrandise itself.

The ferment which these events created led Spanish Christian intellectuals to devote much of their attention to a set of economic circumstances which was quite unlike those of medieval Europe. Among the leading figures in the new lines of economic enquiry were: Francisco de Vitoria (1480–1546); Domingo de Soto (1494–1560); Martin Azplicueta Navarrus (1493–1586); Diego De Covarrubias Y Levia (1512–1577); Luis Molina (1536–1600); Domingo de Banez (1528–1604); and, Juan de Lugo (1583–1623).[36] Each of these were scholastics, and the outward forms of their treatises are in the conventional mould. However, their economic analyses are highly innovative when compared with those of St. Thomas Aquinas and other theologians and jurists of the high middle ages.[37]

What were the bases for this innovative economic analysis? Undoubtedly, one basis was the novelty of the macro-economic circumstances of their era. However, it is also clear that when the Spanish doctors came to address the workings of the contemporary Spanish economy in the face of change, they were obliged to penetrate the micro-economics of a variety of business dealings which centuries of Jewish and Moslem practice had normalized in that country.

For example, the scholastics moralists were obliged to investigate "dry exchange", a contract which disguised lending at interest by means of an international exchange-deal. Another device which required attention was the *mohatra*, or double-contract. A third instance was *census*, a contract which obliges payment of an annual return from fruitful property. As a result of investigation of these and other arrangements prevalent in a Spanish economy in revolution, the schoolmen re-vamped the tradition of Christian economic thought to which they were heirs. Yet, as Grice-Hutchinson points out, in Spain, "we find discussed among Christians, as late as the seventeenth century, typically scholastic problems that had been thrashed out among Jews and Moslems long before."[38]

It may be that in the evolution of Spanish economic thought we will find one of the main conduits through which talmudic economic thought flowed on into the West. Certainly, aspects of the

---

[36] A pioneering investigation of the thought of these and some of their contemporaries is, M. Grice-Hutchinson, *The School of Salamance: Readings in Spanish Monetary Theory, 1544–1605* (Oxford: Clarendon Press, 1952).

[37] For detail, see, B. Gordon, op. cit., pp. 212–7; 236–43.

[38] M. Grice-Hutchinson, *Early Economic Thought in Spain*, p. 14.

economic thought of the Spanish jurists flowed on into the Protestant natural law tradition which eventually influenced Adam
Smith, and the ideas of some Continental economists may have
been even more directly linked to those of these renaissance
schoolmen.[39] The linkages back in time to the talmudists remain
more uncertain. One of the reasons for this uncertainty is an
unfortunate gap in scholarship. Four decades ago, Salo Baron
regretted that "modern historigraphy has been dominated by two
independent lines of investigation, cultivated by medieval historians on the one hand, and by students of Hebrew literature on the
other, and even now the intermingling of the two streams is but in
its incipient stages."[40] It is only by the intermingling to which
Baron looked forward that some of the answers to the queries posed
in this chapter can begin to emerge.

---

[39] On these themes, see, e.g., ibid., pp. 107–15.
[40] S.W. Baron, op. cit., p. 241.

SELECT BIBLIOGRAPHY OF RELATED STUDIES

This compilation lists English-language publications bearing upon the Talmudic treatment of economic issues. Not all of these publications are studies in the history of economic analysis. However, each of them deals with one or more of the themes relevant to research in this particular field.

Agus, Irving A. *Urban Civilization in Pre-Crusade Europe*. New York, Yeshiva University Press, 1965. 821p.

Avi-Yonah, M. "The economics by Byzantine Palestine", *Israel Exploration Journal*, 8 (1958), 39–51.

Baron, Salo W. "The economic views of Maimonides". In his *Essays on Maimonides*. New York, Columbia University Press, 1941, pp. 127–264.

———. "The Economic Factor", in his *The Jewish Factor in Medieval Civilization*, XII (New York, 1942), pp. 18–24.

———. "Capitalism and the Jewish Fate", *The Menorah Journal*, XXX (July–September, 1942).

———. "Economic transformations". In his *A Social and Religious History of the Jews, Volume Four*. New York, Columbia University Press, 1957, pp. 150–227.

———. *Ancient and Medieval Jewish History*. New Brunswick, Rutgers University Press, 1972.

Brooks, R. *Support of the Poor in the Mishnaic Law of Agriculture: Tractate Peah*. Brown Judaic Studies, No. 43. Chico: California, Scholars' Press, 1983, 211p.

Blidstein, G.J. "The Sale of Animals to Gentiles in Talmudic Law", *Jewish Quarterly Review*, 61 (1971) 188–98.

Buchler, A. *The Economic Conditions of Judea After the Destruction of the Second Temple*. London, Jews' College Publications, No. 4, 1912. 63p.

Cohen, Boaz. "Antichresis in Jewish and Roman law". In *Alexander Marx Jubilee Volume*. New York, Jewish Theological Seminary of America, 1950, pp. 179–202.

———. "Usufructus in Jewish and Roman law", *Revue Internationale des Droits de l'Antiquite*, 1 (1954), 173–93.

David, A. Ben. "Jewish and Roman bronze and copper coins: their reciprocal relations in Mishnah and Talmud from Herod the Great to Trajan and Hadrian", *Palestine Exploration Quarterly*, 103 (1971), 109–29.

Gamoran, Hillel. "Talmudic Controls on the Purchases of Futures", *Jewish Quarterly Review*, 64 (1973) 48–66.

———. "Talmudic Usury Laws and Business Loans", *Journal for the Study of Judaism*, 7 (1976) 129–43.

———. "The Talmudic Law of Mortgages in View of the Prohibition against Lending on Interest", *Hebrew Union College Annual*, 52 (1981) 153–62.

Gerber, Haim. "Jews and Money-lending in the Ottoman Empire", *Jewish Quarterly Review*, 72 (1981) 100–18.

Gordon, Barry. "Three Legal Traditions: Rabbis, Romans and Canonists". In his *Economic Analysis Before Adam Smith: Hesiod to Lessius*. London, Macmillan, 1975, pp. 111–152.

Grice-Hutchinson, M. *Early Economic Thought in Spain, 1177–1704*. London, Allen and Unwin, 1978.

Gross, Nachum. Editor. *Economic History of the Jews*. New York, Schocken, 1975. 304p.

Haas, P.J. *A History of the Mishnaic Law of Agriculture*. Brown Judaic Studies No. 18. Chico: California, Scholars' Press, 1980. 222p.

Heinemann, Josef H. "The status of the labourer in Jewish law and society in the Tannaitic period [70 AD–200AD]", *Hebrew Union College Annual*, 25 (1954), 263–325.

Herford, R. Travers. *Talmud and Apocrypha: a comparative study of the Jewish ethical teaching in the rabbinical and non-rabbinical sources in the early centuries.* 1933. New York, Ktav, 1971.

Hoenig, S.B. "The Designated Number of Kinds of Labor Prohibited on the Sabbath", *Jewish Quarterly Review*, 68 (1978) 193–208.

———. (ed.). *Solomon Zeitland's Studies in the Early History of Judaism.* Vol. IV. New York, KTAV, 1978.

Jackson, B.S. "Foreign influence in early Jewish law of theft", *Revue Internationale des Droits de l'Antiquite*, 18 (1971), 25–42.

Jackson, Bernard S. *Theft in Early Jewish Law.* London, Oxford University Press, 1972. 316p.

Jacobs, L. "The economic conditions of the Jews in Babylon in Talmudic times compared with Palestine", *Journal of Semitic Studies*, 2 (1957), 349–59.

Jaffee, M.S. *Mishnah's Theology of Tithing: a Study of Tractate Maaserot.* Brown Judaic Studies No. 19. Chico: California, Scholars' Press, 1981. 214p.

Jung, Leo. "Judaism and the new world order", *American Journal of Economics and Sociology*, 3 (1945) 385–93, and 4 (1945) 515–28.

———. *The Rabbis and the Ethics of Business.* New York, Soncino Press, 1964.

Kadman, L. "The monetary development of Palestine in the light of coin hoards". In A. Kindler (ed.) *Proceedings of the International Numismatic Convention, Jerusalem, 1963.* Tel Aviv, 1967, pp. 311–21.

Kahane, Yehuda. "Modern management parallels in ancient law", *Risk Management* (January 1980), 29–37.

Kleiman, Ephraim. "An early modern Hebrew textbook of Economics", *History of Political Economy*, 5 (1973), 339–358.

———. "Bi-Metallism in Rabbi's Time: Two Variants of the Mishna 'Gold Acquires Silver,'" *Zion*, 38 (1973), 48–61.

———. "Markets and Fairs in the Land of Israel in the Period of the Mishnah and the Talmud", *Zion*, 51 (1986), 472–86.

———. "Just price in Talmudic literature", *History of Political Economy*, 19 (1987), 23–45.

———. "Opportunity cost, human capital, and some related economic concepts in talmudic literature", *History of Political Economy*, 19 (1987), 261–287.

———. *Public Finance Criteria in the Talmud.* Jerusalem, Hebrew University, Department of Economics Working Paper, No. 192, June 1988. 40p.

Leister, Burton M. "The Rabbinic Tradition and Corporate Morality", in, Oliver Williams and John Houck (eds.), *The Judeo-Christian Vision and the Modern Corporation.* Notre Dame and London, University of Notre Dame Press, 1982, pp. 141–58.

Levine, A. "Opportunity costs as treated in Talmudic literature", *Tradition*, 15 (1975), 153–72.

———. *Free Enterprise and Jewish Law.* New York, 1980.

Lieberman, Saul. *Hellenism in Jewish Palestine.* New York, Jewish Theological Seminary of America, 1950.

Liebermann, Yehoshua, "Elements of Talmudic monetary thought", *History of Political Economy*, 11 (1979), 254–70.

———. "Origins of Coase's theorem in Jewish law", *Journal of Legal Studies* (1981), 293–303.

———. "The economics of Kethubah valuation", *History of Political Economy*, 15 (1983), 519–28.

Maloney, Robert P. "Usury in Greek, Roman and Rabbinic thought", *Traditio*, 27 (1971) 79–109.

Mandelbaum, Irving. *A History of the Mishnaic Law of Agriculture.* Chico: Scholars' Press, 1982.

Moore, George F. *Judaism in the First Centuries of the Christian Era.* Cambridge, Mass., Harvard University Press, 1927.

Newman, L.E. *The Sanctity of the Seventh Year: a Study of Mishnah Tractate Shebit.* Brown Judaic Studies No. 44. Chico: California, Scholars' Press, 1983. 267p.

Niditch, S. "The Cosmic Adam: Man as Mediator in Rabbinic Literature", *Journal of Jewish Studies*, 34 (1983) 137–46.

Ohrenstein, Roman A. "Economic Thought in Talmudic Literature in the Light of Modern Economics", *American Journal of Economics and Sociology*, 27 (1968), 185–96.

————. "Economic Self-interest and Social Progress in Talmudic literature", *American Journal of Economics and Sociology*, 29 (1970), 59–69.

————. "Economic Aspects of Organized Religion in Perspective: The Early Phase", *Nassau Review*, (Spring 1970), 27–43.

————. "Economic Aspects of Organized Religion: Perspective and Analysis of the Modern phase", *Nassau Review* (Spring 1971), 37–61.

————. "Economic Analysis in Talmudic Literature: Some Ancient Studies of Value", *American Journal of Economics and Sociology*, 38 (1979). Abstract only. Monograph in Microfiche, American Association for Information Science.

————. "Some Studies of Value in Talmudic Literature in the Light of Modern Economics", *Nassau Review*, 4 (1981), 48–70.

————. "Value Analysis in Talmudic Literature in the Light of Modern Economics", *International Review of Economics and Ethics*, 1 (1986), 34–52.

————. "Game Theory in the Talmud: An Economic Perspective", *International Journal of Social Economics*, 16, No. 7, 1989.

————. and B. Gordon, "Some Aspects of Human Capital in Talmudic Literature", *International Journal of Social Economics*, 14 (1987), 185–90. First published as Research Report or Occasional Paper No. 120, University of New-castle, Department of Economics, August 1985.

————. and B. Gordon, "Quantitative Dimensions of Human Capital Analysis in the Talmudic Tradition", *International Journal of Social Economics*, 16 (1989), 5–13.

Pollins, Harold. *Economic History of the Jews in England.* London and Toronto, Associated University Presses, 1982, 339p.

Priest, J.E. *Governmental and Judicial Ethics in the Bible and Rabbinic Literature.* New York, KTAV, 1980. 313p.

Rackmann, E. "A Jewish Philosophy of Property: Rabbinic Insights on Intestate Succession", *Jewish Quarterly Review*, 67 (1976–77) 65–89.

Reich, Nathan. "Capitalism and the Jews", *The Menorah Journal*, 13 (January 1930).

Roscher, W. "The status of the Jews in the middle ages considered from the standpoint of commercial policy", *Historia Judaica*, 6 (1944), 13–26.

Rosenthal, Gilbert S. *Banking and Finance Among Jews in Renaissance Italy.* New York, 1962.

Safrai, Shemuel. "Monetary development in the third and fourth centuries as reflected in Talmudic literature". In A. Kindler (ed.) *Proceedings of the International Numismatic Conference Jerusalem, 1963.* Tel Aviv, 1967, pp. 251–9.

Sarson, R.S. *A History of the Mishnaic Law of Agriculture.* Leiden, Brill, 1979. 189p.

Shapiro, Aharon. "Rabbinical response and the regulation of competition", in *American Journal of Economics and Sociology*, 29 (1970), 71–6.

————. "The poverty program of Judaism", *Review of Social Economy*, 29 (1971), 200–6.

Silver, M. "Karl Polanyi and markets in the ancient near east", *Journal of Economic History*, 43 (1983), 795–829.

————. *Economic Structures of the Ancient Near East.* London and Sydney, Croom Helm, 1985.

Sombart, Werner. *The Jews and Modern Capitalism.* London, Fisher, 1913.

Sperber, Daniel. "On social and economic conditions in third century Palestine", *Archiv Orientali*, 38 (1970), 1–25.

———. "Costs of living in Roman Palestine", *Journal of the Economic and Social History of the Orient*, 13 (1970), 1–15. (See also, 8 (1965), 248–71; 9 (1966), 182–211).

———. *Roman Palestine, 200–400: Money and Prices*. Ramat-Gan, Bar-Ilan University, 1974. 331p.

———. *Roman Palestine, 200–400: the Land*. Ramat-Gan, Bar-Ilan University, 1978.

Starr, Joshua. *The Jews in the Byzantine Empire, 641–1204*. Athens, Verlag Der 'Byzantinish-Neugriechischen Jahrbucher', 1939. 266p.

Stein, Seigfried. "The development of Jewish law on interest from the biblical period to the expulsion of the Jews from England", *Historia Judaica*, 17 (1955), 3–40.

———. "Interest taken by Jews from Gentiles: an evaluation of source material (14th to 17th centuries)", *Journal of Semitic Studies*, 1 (1956), 141–66.

Urbach, E.E. "The laws regarding slavery as a source for social history of the period of the Second Temple, the Mishnah and Talmud". In J.G. Weiss (ed.) *Papers of the Institute of Jewish Studies. Volume One*. Jerusalem, 1964, pp. 1–94.

Zeitlin, Solomon. "Slavery during the Second Commonwealth and the Tannaitic period", *Jewish Quarterly Review*, 53 (1962), 185–218.

———. "Studies in Talmudic jurisprudence. I: possession, pignus and hypothec", *Jewish Quarterly Review*, 60 (1969–70), 89–111.

NAME INDEX

SUBJECT INDEX

152 SUBJECT INDEX

Palestine 3–4
Pesharah 75–82
Pharisees 5–6
Poel Botel 60
poor, the 22, 27–9
population 16–7, 108
price 30–2, 48–51, 64–6, 121
priests 27–8, 31–2, 36, 40, 67, 108–9, 118, 120
production 20–3, 26, 41–3, 46
productivity 30–2, 106–7, 118–9, 121–3, 127
profit 19, 61–4, 86, 97, 134, 138
prosperity 19, 47–50, 53
Providence 42–5
puritanism xiv, 137–8

risk 69, 74, 83–97
Rubba 10–12

sabbath 21–2
sabbatical year 22–5, 53, 127
Sadducees 6
Sages 6, 11, 65, 73, 81
sale 12, 30, 61–4, 133
Sanhedrin 6, 10, 35–6, 53
scarcity 19, 46–7, 49, 59–60
Scribes (*Sopherim*) 5–6
self-interest xiii, 19, 35–45, 69
Sinai 4, 9, 27
S'khar B'teilo 57–9
slaves 22, 24–5, 31, 70, 111, 114, 121–2, 126–7, 133
socialism 138–9
solar activity 51–3
soul 38, 102, 104
Spain xiv, xv, 140–3

strangers 22, 28, 30
sugya 10
supply 47–8, 51

Tabernacle 115–8
Talmud
  majority rule in 9–12, 14
  method 7–12, 71–2, 84
  origins 4–6, 14
  structure 3–4, 37
Tannaim 3, 5
Temple 5–6, 27, 32, 35, 66, 116, 118
tithes 26, 28–9, 67
Torah (Pentateuch) ix, xvii, 4–6, 15, 58, 123
Tovath Hanoah 91–4

uncertainty 68–9, 83–97
United States xiv, 138
usury 105, 132–4, 136
utility 18, 41, 61, 103, 106–7, 109, 125

valuation 90–4, 103–13, 120–2
value xi, 8, 30–2, 101–13, 121–2, 127–8
valueless value xiii, 101, 110–3, 125–8
virtue 36, 38–41, 47

wages 29, 31, 36, 59–61, 119
war 26, 70–1
wealth (riches) 18–20, 29–30, 36, 41
Wisdom tradition xiii, xvii, 14–20, 88–9, 116–7, 119
work 21–2, 31, 43–4, 46, 61, 106, 116–7, 119

Yetzer-Ha-rah 37–9

Zeyoona 87–8, 97

BY THE SAME AUTHORS

ROMAN A. OHRENSTEIN:
  Inventories During Business Fluctuations
  Inventory Control as an Economic Shock Absorber
    (Supplemental Essay in Hebrew)

BARRY GORDON:
  Non-Ricardian Political Economy
  Economic Analysis Before Adam Smith
  Political Economy in Parliament
  Economic Doctrine and Tory Liberalism
  The Economic Problem in Biblical and Patristic
    Thought

STUDIA POST-BIBLICA

1. KOSMALA, H. *Hebräer - Essener - Christen*. Studien zur Vorgeschichte der frühchristlichen Verkündigung. 1959. ISBN 90 04 02135 3
3. WEISE, M. *Kultzeiten und kultischer Bundesschluss in der 'Ordensregel' vom Toten Meer*. 1961. ISBN 90 04 02136 1
4. VERMES, G. *Scripture and Tradition in Judaism*. Haggadic Studies. Reprint. 1983. ISBN 90 04 07096 6
5. CLARKE, E.G. *The Selected Questions of Isho bar Nūn on the Pentateuch*. Edited and Translated from Ms Cambridge Add. 2017. With a Study of the Relationship of Isho'dādh of Merv, Theodore bar Konī and Isho bar Nūn on Genesis. 1962. ISBN 90 04 03141 3
6. NEUSNER, J. *A Life of Yohanan ben Zakkai (ca. 1-80 C.E.)*. 2nd rev. ed. 1970. ISBN 90 04 02138 8
7. WEIL, G.E. *Élie Lévita, humaniste et massorète (1469-1549)*. 1963. ISBN 90 04 02139 6
8. BOWMAN, J. *The Gospel of Mark*. The New Christian Jewish Passover Haggadah. 1965. ISBN 90 04 03142 1
10. MORGENSTERN, J. *Some significant Antecedents of Christianity*. 1966. ISBN 90 04 02142 6
11. NEUSNER, J. *A History of the Jews in Babylonia*. Part 2. The Early Sasanian Period. 1966. ISBN 90 04 02143 4
12. NEUSNER, J. Part 3. From Shapur I to Shapur II. 1968. ISBN 90 04 02144 2
14. NEUSNER, J. Part 4. The Age of Shapur II. 1969. ISBN 90 04 02146 9
15. NEUSNER, J. Part 5. Later Sasanian Times. 1970. ISBN 90 04 02147 7
16. NEUSNER, J. *Development of a Legend*. Studies on the Traditions Concerning Yohanan ben Zakkai. 1970. ISBN 90 04 02148 5
17. NEUSNER, J. (ed.). *The Formation of the Babylonian Talmud*. Studies in the Achievements of the Late Nineteenth and Twentieth Century Historical and Literary-Critical Research. 1970. ISBN 90 04 02149 3
18. CATCHPOLE, D.R. *The Trial of Jesus*. A Study in the Gospels and Jewish Historiography from 1770 to the Present Day. 1971. ISBN 90 04 02599 5
19. NEUSNER, J. *Aphrahat and Judaism*. The Christian-Jewish Argument in Fourth-Century Iran. 1971. ISBN 90 04 02150 7
20. DAVENPORT, G.L. *The Eschatology of the Book of Jubilees*. 1971. ISBN 90 04 02600 2
21. FISCHEL, H.A. *Rabbinic Literature and Greco-Roman Philosophy*. A Study of Epicurea and Rhetorica in Early Midrashic Writings. 1973. ISBN 90 04 03720 9
22. TOWNER, W.S. *The Rabbinic 'Enumeration of Scriptural Examples'*. A Study of a Rabbinic Pattern of Discourse with Special Reference to *Mekhilta d'Rabbi Ishmael*. 1973. ISBN 90 04 03744 6
23. NEUSNER, J. (ed.). *The Modern Study of the Mishna*. 1973. ISBN 90 04 03669 5
24. ASMUSSEN, J.P. *Studies in Judeo-Persian Literature*. [Tr. from the Danish]. (Homages et Opera Minora, 12). 1973. ISBN 90 04 03827 2
25. BARZILAY, I. *Yoseph Shlomo Delmedigo (Yashar of Candia)*. His Life, Works and Times. 1974. ISBN 90 04 03972 4
26. PSEUDO-JEROME. *Quaestiones on the Book of Samuel*. Edited with an Introduction by A. Saltman. 1975. ISBN 90 04 04195 8

27. BERGER, K. *Die griechische Daniel-Diegese*. Eine altkirchliche Apokalypse. Text, Übersetzung und Kommentar. 1976. ISBN 90 04 04756 5

28. LOWY, S. *The Principles of Samaritan Bible Exegesis*. 1977. ISBN 90 04 04925 8

29. DEXINGER, F. *Henochs Zehnwochenapokalypse und offene Probleme der Apokalyptik-forschung*. 1977. ISBN 90 04 05428 6

30. COHEN, J.M. *A Samaritan Chronicle*. A Source-Critical Analysis of the Life and Times of the Great Samaritan Reformer, Baba Rabbah. 1981. ISBN 90 04 06215 7

31. BROADIE, A. *A Samaritan Philosophy*. A Study of the Hellenistic Cultural Ethos of the Memar Marqah. 1981. ISBN 90 04 06312 9

32. HEIDE, A. VAN DER. *The Yemenite Tradition of the Targum of Lamentations*. Critical Text and Analysis of the Variant Readings. 1981. ISBN 90 04 06560 1

33. ROKEAH, D. *Jews, Pagans and Christians in Conflict*. 1982. ISBN 90 04 07025 7

35. EISENMAN, R.H. *James the Just in the Habakkuk Pesher*. 1986. ISBN 90 04 07587 9

36. HENTEN, J.W. VAN, H.J. DE JONGE, P.T. VAN ROODEN & J.W. WEESELIUS (eds.). *Tradition and Re-Interpretation in Jewish and Early Christian Literature*. Essays in Honour of Jürgen C.H. Lebram. 1986. ISBN 90 04 07752 9

37. PRITZ, R.A. *Nazarene Jewish Christianity*. From the End of the New Testament Period until Its Disappearance in the Fourth Century. 1988. ISBN 90 04 08108 9

38. HENTEN, J.W. VAN, B.A.G.M. DEHANDSCHUTTER & H.W. VAN DER KLAAUW. *Die Entstehung der jüdischen Martyrologie*. 1989. ISBN 90 04 08978 0

39. MASON, S. *Flavius Josephus on the Pharisees*. A Composition-Critical Study. 1991. ISBN 90 04 09181 5

40. OHRENSTEIN, R.A. & B. GORDON. *Economic Analysis in Talmudic Literature*. Rabbinic Thought in the Light of Modern Economics. 1992. ISBN 90 04 09540 3